LIVE THE FINER LIFE

LIVE THE FINER LIFE

Financial Independence Never Ever Retire

How to Create and Manage
Your Family's Asset Management Business

PATRICK J. KEOGH

STONEBROOK
PUBLISHING

A STONEBROOK PUBLISHING BOOK
©2023 Patrick J. Keogh

Library of Congress Control Number: 2023909399

Hardcover ISBN: 978-1-955711-25-8

Ebook ISBN: 978-1-955711-26-5

www.stonebrookpublishing.net

PRINTED IN THE UNITED STATES OF AMERICA

Other Titles by Patrick J. Keogh

- Make Your Family Rich: Why to Replace Retirement Planning with Succession Planning
- Hey Kid! Wanna Own Great American Businesses?
- Federal Government Asset-Backed Financing: Financing a Federal Government Equipment Lease with Gregg A. Day

To Annie and John Keogh (Mom and Pop), the founders of the Make Your Family Rich system. They went long on the United States during the Great Depression when most went the other way. The most successful investors ever. Thank you.

CONTENTS

INTRODUCTION

I LIKE THE WAY PABLO PICASSO SAID IT: "THERE IS only one way to see things until someone shows us how to look with different eyes." With respect to investing, my hope is that this book will serve as those different eyes for you. This book is your blueprint for how to live the FINER life.

Many have heard the acronym FIRE when it comes to all things financial. FIRE stands for Financial Independence Retire Early. There are various strategies promoted by investment managers and analysts to achieve sufficient wealth to live independently and work free into your retirement. The FIRE idea heralds retirement as the ideal destination achieved by creating a financially successful life—and the sooner you get to retirement, the better.

From reading various business and investment publications and watching financial presentations on television and online, I've noticed that a great deal of attention is focused on achieving a secure retirement. It seems like retirement is the single most important objective of successful investing. Retirement tends to be all about escaping the daily grind, maybe some golf and fishing, traveling, and spending quality time with family and friends—all without any financial worry. It's on television every day. Many periodicals regularly run articles with titles like "The 10 Best Places to Retire." You get the picture.

My objective is for you to see things with those different eyes that Picasso had in mind.

The purpose of this book is to introduce our readers to the FINER life. That stands for Financial Independence Never Ever Retire. Now calm down. That doesn't mean you'll never be able to kick back and relax or move on from that nine-to-five job. You can do all the things those conventional retirees are doing. It *does* mean that you'll achieve the freedom that results from wealth. But it also means that overseeing your investments, which are the businesses you've accumulated, will become your business. Throughout this book, we call the investments you have accumulated, own, and manage your "asset management business."

Think about Warren Buffett for a minute. As of this writing, Buffett is ninety-two and is overseeing a wide range of public and private companies. The guy looks and sounds great, and he gets to hang out with all the cool folks. One of the wealthiest people in the world, he decides when and how much time and energy he devotes to work. His friends, heirs, and investors spend a lot of time wondering who will succeed him as manager of the wide array of businesses that is Berkshire Hathaway today.

Think of Berkshire Hathaway as Buffett's asset management business. Warren Buffett is living the FINER life, running all the businesses he's accumulated over his lifetime and concentrating on training his successors to take over. Buffett does not work for the business. The business works for him. That's what this book will show you how to do. This book will show you how your asset management business can be developed and structured to work for you and your successors.

Sometimes it seems like the entire financial services industry is geared toward designing the ideal retirement strategy. That strategy involves a focus on what? Well, one fellow on TV always says the worst thing that can happen in retirement is to "run out of money." Now there's a grand, lofty objective. Look, there are lots of things worse than running out of money in retirement. How about a child with special medical or schooling needs? Or a grandchild with a chronic disease or drug addiction? A spouse or sibling dealing with an early onset of a mental disability? Those things will require a loved one with the time to help and the wealth to fund whatever may be necessary. This book will help you plan for that kind of empowerment.

Like Buffett, this book will help you design your succession plan. Not a *retirement* plan but a *succession* plan. A succession plan that determines who will succeed you in managing the asset management businesses you have assembled. I will detail how and when you train those who will work with you in operating your asset management business and eventually take over from you one day. That could be your children, grandchildren, or other family members. It could be special friends or a charitable institution, or maybe even a university endowment that will succeed you.

This book and its principles will be the training manual for both you as the founder of your business and your successors. As the saying goes, "You don't get the valuables until the values are successfully transferred." That's how I see it. I don't simply want to pass on and then have my heirs divvy up the assets that took me all these years to develop. I want them to see, understand, and succeed to my asset management business with the full knowledge of how to run it, at least as well as the old man did. In my case, I think they will do it better.

You may consider the principles promoted in this book as unconventional. In fact, financial advisors have told me they could never recommend some of these principles—not necessarily because they don't believe in them but because their lawyers would never let them.

I've been investing since my teen years, and it took me a long time to figure out how to formulate my family's and my asset management business. I made all the mistakes and often the same mistake multiple times while listening to others—those experts. I stuck with it; some things worked, and over time, I put together what we call the Make Your Family Rich (MYFR) system, first detailed in my earlier book by the same title. That's our system. It works great for us, and we think it will work for you too. It's a do-it-yourself approach based on the MYFR principles.

The MYFR system is what we call the approach to achieve your FINER life. For the last twenty years or so, we have refined and applied the MYFR system with solid results. Maybe more importantly, my two adult children, who are my primary successors, believe in and now administer much of the MYFR system for our family. I wrote a second book titled *Hey Kid! Wanna Own Great American Businesses?* targeted at the younger business owner. That book is being used to train my grandchildren, and like *Make Your Family Rich; Why to Replace Retirement Planning with Succession Planning*, it's available from Amazon and Barnes and Noble. Better yet, order through our website, www.makeyourfamilyrich.com.

In this book, I'll first present in summary fashion the principles of the MYFR system. These are the various building blocks of the system. The chapters that follow will delve more deeply into each of those guiding principles and the rationale for their inclusion in the system. I also share my personal and family backgrounds and experience leading up to the MYFR system. That will be followed by the details of the current management of our asset management business and our succession planning.

I hope you find the MYFR system a very common-sense approach to investing and creating your family's asset management business. You will not find a lot of formulas, Latin and Greek terms, and graphs on these pages. I will not try to teach you fundamental financial analysis to get at those undiscovered bargains. The purpose of this book is not to teach you how to become a Wall Street analyst. The purpose is to communicate the common sense I acquired over a lifetime of mistakes. My hope is to get my readers to my ultimate business investing destination, which is the MYFR system, but to get you there sooner and without all those costly mistakes. The tools are readily and mostly freely available, and I will show you how to access all that data. Mazel tov!

1

VOCABULARY

WORDS MATTER IN ALL THINGS. THE WORDS you use can affect the way you think. Jonathan Swift wrote that "Words are the clothing of our thoughts." Here are a few introductory comments about the use of vocabulary in this book. Vocabulary is very important in our investment approach. We will mostly depart from the standard wording of investing.

This book is about investing in *businesses*. Businesses are where folks work to create things and value for their fellow citizens, consumers, and owners. Businesses are also where we and our neighbors work and earn the livings that support our families. Businesses and those folks who work there help us accumulate wealth to make our families rich and independent. We try not to focus on or write a lot about *stocks*. Stocks, to us, seem to imply an impersonal, transitory interest. Stock is simply the evidence of our ownership in our businesses. When we own stock in a business, it is *our business,* and the folks who work there are *our people,* and the stuff they make and sell, that's *our stock in trade*. We own that business, and we plan to own it forever. Like any business owner, we patronize our businesses and encourage our friends and family to also support the businesses we own.

Stocks are things that are *traded,* and that currency is used to *play the market.* We don't advocate trading, and we certainly don't think of owning our businesses as playing the market. Owning our businesses is not a game. It's a serious matter about investing in the businesses we own, as well as the people who make those businesses work, create wealth, and reward their employees and owners. We are proud of the businesses we own. You can have pride in a business that is yours, not so much a stock you own for a short while. I cringe when I hear or read someone say something like, "the five tech stocks to play now with the coming recession."

You will not see phrases like "playing the market," "gambling in the stock market," or "Wall Street is a casino" in this book. That's not what the MYFR system is all about. There will always be an element of uncertainty about business investing. But it's not like the uncertainty associated with gambling. We are buying businesses, and there will be risks associated with managing the quality and marketability of the products and all the wide range of factors that make for a successful business. This book will tell you how to select those businesses most likely to be successful over the long term. Those are the businesses you want to own in your asset management business.

There's an important discussion in this book about how to acquire businesses. We rarely buy the business directly. Rather, we use options. The thought of trading options scares many people, and for good reason. Options can be complex and risky. The way we recommend you use options is smart and safe. The challenge for many people is in the *vocabulary* of options. We will try to explain our use of options in poolroom English. We deal with options in detail in Chapter 5, "Sell the Dips; Out-of-the-Money *Put Options,* That Is." That's an important topic, and once you understand the vocabulary of options, you'll realize how easy it will be to trade them and how lucrative their proper use will be in creating your asset management business.

When we talk about our *asset management business,* we mean the aggregate of all the great businesses and assets our family owns. Our asset management business is somewhat like Warren Buffett's Berkshire Hathaway. Our family asset management business owns and manages our interest in a wide array of mostly publicly owned businesses. In another time and with another family, the family business might be a large Italian restaurant or a hardware store, and generations would have worked there in various roles to make the business function and prosper. In our case, businesses have been securitized over my lifetime, and it's easy to separate the investor role from the business manager role. Our family business comprises investments in a wide array of great American public businesses. This book is about how we assembled and continue to manage our family asset management business.

Patrick J. Keogh started our asset management business and wrote this book, but his adult children, Matthew and Erin, run many things now and edited the manuscript of this book. Increasingly, we try to inform and engage the grandchildren in our asset management business. Pat keeps a hand in and a close eye on things, but Matt and Erin meet each day to actually apply the systems and techniques detailed here. So, from time to time, the point of view will switch from *I* to *we* because the various roles in running the business tend to merge. That's as it should be because, in our view of succession, the next generations will spend a lot more time with the family business and its capital than will Pat.

2

THE NINE GUIDING PRINCIPLES OF THE MYFR SYSTEM

THERE ARE NINE GUIDING PRINCIPLES OF THE Make Your Family Rich system. Applying these principles to the creation of your asset management business is the foundation for achieving the FINER life. Many of the principles will fly in the face of more conventional rules espoused by your standard investment advisors. Many of the MYFR principles will warrant a chapter of their own to explain the rationale for the principle and how it fits into the development of your family's asset management business. For now, this is a summary. Try to get an understanding of how the principles meld into the larger MYFR system and reserve judgment on the validity of each principle until you read the fuller explanation further along in the book. Try to stay receptive to seeing things with different eyes.

1. Measure your performance and success by the income you earn, not the value of your portfolio of businesses.
That's right, every investment "expert" says you should focus on the value of what you own. You need to compare your portfolio's performance against various market standards or indices. Markets will go up, and markets will go down; you can't control any of that.

However, you can control the income your asset management business generates, and this book will explain how. The MYFR system measures performance by income and will ensure your income reliably goes up—and only up—over time. You will always want to know the market value of your asset management business, but you will make decisions primarily on the constantly increasing income from your business, not the current and often volatile market value of your investments.

2. Invest only in Dividend Champions.

These are mostly the great American businesses that have increased the income or dividends to their owners for a minimum of twenty-five years. Go long on America and only America.

As of this writing, there are about 143 Dividend Champions. Almost all are American-based, though there are a few with headquarters in other countries like Canada and Ireland. But the bulk of revenue for even these few businesses is in the US. Do you want global exposure or participation in emerging markets? Many of the Dividend Champions have a whole lot of foreign sales, but they are based and regulated in the good old US of A. With your income constantly increasing, the urge to sell in those inevitable steep market declines will be vastly reduced. We call that controlling the gnu in you.

3. Don't Buy the Dips; Sell the Dips. That's out-of-the-money put options.

Standard investment advice is to buy market dips. Do you like a particular company? Then, when the price dips, you'll like it even more, so go ahead and buy it. The MYFR system will encourage you to sell puts on Dividend Champions on any day when the underlying Dividend Champion dips significantly in the market. You're going to learn to love this technique and the additional income its use will generate.

4. DRIP as much as you can of your dividend income.
DRIP stands for Dividend Reinvestment Plan, which is the means for reinvesting your dividends by buying an increasing interest in each Dividend Champion. If you do not currently need the income, you should DRIP your dividends. It's the way to turbocharge the power of compounding interest.

5. Engage your successors early in the development and management of your asset management business and pay them to train and operate the business.
Whether it's your children or other family member, friends, or your charities, you need to expose your successors as soon as possible to the MYFR system. They need to fully understand and buy into the logic, techniques, and objectives of the MYFR system. You also need to compensate them for their time and work as they grow into more active roles in managing your asset management business.

6. Never sell as long as your Dividend Champions continue to increase their dividends. If they fail to increase their dividends, then prepare to sell.
If a Dividend Champion stops increasing its dividend, then your primary reason for acquiring that business is gone. There are better ways than others for disposing of the business, but disposing is what you need to do. We will show you how best to exit a former Dividend Champion using option-selling techniques.

7. If you need to scratch an itch, do it, but in moderation.
We recognize that limiting your acquisitions to Dividend Champions may feel a bit rigid and restraining. If you have special knowledge of other businesses and have the urge to buy them, then do so, but do it in moderation. We call those Scratch the Itch (STI) investments.

8. Move to the rich neighborhood.
We mean that virtually. That is, successful, rich people have patterns of behavior in the things they do and what they read. You should be doing those things, too. They also have habits and practices they avoid, and you should avoid those as well.

9. Retirement? Fergedaboudit! You will evolve into owning and managing your family's asset management business.
That's right; you simply will evolve into the chairman of the board who oversees your family's asset management business. You'll have all the time and money you need to do that conventional retirement stuff if that's what you want. But you can also continue to interact with your successors. My bet is that you'll prefer that interaction to playing golf. But, hey, you can do both!

3

EARLY YEARS, EDUCATION, AND VALUES

WITH LIMITED EXCEPTION, MY EARLIEST investing was in real estate. I thought I did well at that, but my real estate investing was more about running a business than investing. For some time now, in developing and employing the Make Your Family Rich system, I've migrated to being an investor almost exclusively and am focused *only* on the investor role. I leave managing the business aspects of my investments to the professionals who run our public businesses. During my lifetime, investing opportunities became much more securitized, efficient, analytical, and professional. I hope that you will bypass investing in hands-on businesses much earlier than I did.

The Bronx Boy and Education

I was born, raised, and educated in the Bronx. During the Carter Administration, I learned that I lived in the *South* Bronx. That's how the President referred to my neighborhood. *South* apparently meant it was poorer than the regular Bronx. We had no sense of that at the time.

My parents were always superintendents of the buildings we lived in. Those are the folks who manage and maintain the apartment buildings. We lived rent-free in the basement, and my mother and father did most of the work to take care of the tenants and the building. That pretty much included everything from keeping the building clean, collecting and putting out the trash, mopping the halls, renting the units, and collecting the rent. In addition to being a super, my father had another full-time job. As the super, he also picked up odd jobs helping the tenants with other projects. My mother focused on raising the children and doing the super's job.

I've never known harder-working, more family- and education-focused people than my parents. Being a super was a way to access affordable housing in one of the most expensive cities in the world. Today, governments have affordable housing programs. Back then, Mom and Pop exchanged their labor for housing.

All the children—and there were four of us—went to Catholic elementary and high schools. My sister married shortly after high school and did not continue to college. In that place and time, it was somewhat of an exception for a young woman to pursue higher education. In fact, including college and graduate school, I attended male-only schools.

The exception was in my third year at Georgetown's night law school when women were introduced to all classes. Law school was very competitive, and every student knew his class rank. We resisted the introduction of women, not for any sexist reason, but because we believed the administration would only admit the most successful female students, thereby adversely affecting our class rankings. Today, like at my undergraduate school, Manhattan College, most of the students and graduates at Georgetown Law are women.

My parents paid the tuition for our education up to college, and then we were expected to work part-time and help with the college costs. Tuition costs had to be a burden for Mom and Pop, and therein lay the need for so much work. Early on, we didn't think much of their sacrifice, and they never complained. Both my parents were immigrants with limited education, and I never doubted that our education was their priority or that they would earn the funds necessary to pay for school—no matter what.

Growing up in the Bronx, most of my contemporaries were the sons and daughters of immigrants. In our area of the Bronx, the adults were predominantly either Italian, Irish, or Jewish. The Jews were either from Eastern Europe or Russia, and their children went to public schools. Most of the Italian and Irish were Catholic, and their children went to Catholic schools. Many of the teachers in Catholic schools seemed to be of Irish descent.

Discipline in school—and particularly the Catholic schools— was strict and included corporal punishment. No one thought much about that; certainly, our parents did not. It was just the way it was. School, both Catholic and public, was very competitive, and the quality of education was outstanding. I think that was because the educational expectations of all the immigrant parents were uniformly high. Mind you, none of the families had much money, but the schools were terrific because the parents set such high educational expectations on both the schools and their children.

I kind of choke today when I hear folks expressing their views on contemporary educational philosophy. For example, it's common now to hear that "educators should not teach to the test." Given my background, that idea seems insane to me. Of course, you should teach to the test! How else will you know the student learned the material unless he or she does well on the test? Then there is the disdain for memorizing. Today, educators promote creative thinking rather than rote memorizing. Nonsense, in my book. Students should memorize the facts of American history, for example, and be able to demonstrate their knowledge by doing well on history and civics tests.

In my time, the percentage of males going on to college was surprisingly high, given the economic class. New York state offered both scholarships and loans, and though no one had much money, everyone found a way. In my case, although I worked and saved money for school, I borrowed the money interest-free from a New York state program. Why would I borrow? I did mention it was interest-free, right? I paid for tuition and books with my earned money, and I invested using my borrowed funds. I could sign for my loans, but I started college at seventeen, and when I tried to buy my first stock, I was rejected for being underage. I had to get my older brother, Mike, to open the account in his name and buy the stock I selected. I was old enough to borrow but not old enough to invest. Go figure. Upon graduation, I sold the stock and paid off the loans before interest could accrue. Borrowing and investing back then with no knowledge and experience was one of the crazier things I did, and I sure wouldn't encourage young folks to do that today.

Fortunately, it worked out for me.

Early Work Experience

My brother, Mike, and I worked through high school and college for the concessions at sports venues around New York City, like Yankee Stadium, Shea Stadium, and the Polo Grounds. The concessions were run by Harry M. Stevens Inc. Harry was supposedly the inventor of the hot dog. My younger brother, John, had a variety of jobs during school to help with his education costs. We all lived at home through college or until we married, as in my sister's case.

Working in the ballparks was a great start to my working life. In New York City, you could not be formally employed until the age of fourteen, when you could qualify for what they called "working papers." As soon as we hit fourteen, we applied for papers, and Mike and I went to work at the ballparks. The job was a straight up commission position. That is, you showed up on game day and submitted your papers, and the boss called out the names of the people he needed for the game. He started with the most senior, and early on, you might not get picked on a slow day. But if you kept showing up, eventually, you'd get selected and start building seniority.

Once selected, you were assigned a commodity like soda, ice cream, peanuts, hot dogs, and, if you were at least eighteen years old, beer. It was a hunt-kill-eat job. That is, the vendor earned 12.5%, or one-eighth, of whatever he sold. Though we were formally vendors, we called ourselves hustlers. And that's what we did: hustle. There was no minimum wage, and if it was a small crowd or a cold day, and you were selling ice cream, tough luck. There was only one approach, and it was to run up and down the aisles to make whatever sales you could. There were very few tips. We called them subways, though I never knew the origins of the term. Running up and down those Yankee Stadium aisles for a doubleheader in July or August kept a hustler in shape. You could lose fifteen pounds in a day just by sweating.

Early Entrepreneurial Ventures

I started working in the ballparks at a bad time. It was just after the Giants and Dodgers moved to California and before the advent of the Mets. So work was limited to the Yankees, and that was not enough to keep me fully engaged or generate the income I needed to live and save for school. That's when I started my own independent retail operation at about age fifteen. The following disclosures will eliminate any remaining hope I have for appointment to the Supreme Court, but here it goes.

You see, I opened my own retail fireworks enterprise. Fireworks are illegal in New York City, but they are also popular, and the margins were solid. The sale of fireworks is also one of those victimless crimes, right? Like other activities, including various street sports, fireworks had seasons back then. There was a season for football and a season for stickball. There was a season for linoleum guns and a season for scooters. We made the linoleum guns out of boxes and rubber bands, and they shot squares of linoleum. Scooters were milk boxes on a two-by-four propelled by old skates. Seasons happened about the same time each year, and there was no start or finish but some sort of social contract among the neighborhood children.

The season for fireworks generally started around May each year and had pretty much fizzled out by the Fourth of July. At the start of the fireworks season, I traveled by subway up to Gun Hill Road in the north Bronx. There was a store there that, from the exterior, looked like your standard neighborhood candy store with soda and Breyers ice cream signs in the window. But once inside, there was nothing but a couple of Italian guys sitting behind a table. I told them what I wanted in terms of firecrackers, ash cans, cherry bombs, rockets, and Roman candles. They gave me the prices, and I paid the bill. These were not guys you'd ever want to negotiate with. Once the tab was paid, I was escorted to a vacant lot that was mostly a large rock shaped like a volcano. I'd walk around this huge bolder and into the volcano, and there was my order in brown paper bags. The guy then went over my list, and I was on my own to get back to the subway.

The most popular item was firecrackers. They came in so-called mats of twenty packs, with each pack containing twenty firecrackers. A mat cost $2 wholesale from the Italians. That's ten cents a pack. Most times, I would sell a pack for twenty cents. At the height of the fireworks season, I might get a quarter. I learned the relationship between supply and demand early through my retail business. It was about the same markup for the other items. For example, a cherry bomb cost me a quarter and would retail for fifty cents. There were limited operating expenses other than inventory and the subway fares to Gun Hill Road.

My retail location was on the corner of 165th Street and Summit Avenue in the Highbridge section of the Bronx. Guys would come up and tell me what they wanted, and when they gave me the money, I'd retrieve the merchandise from wherever I had it hidden—kind of like the Italian candy store merchandising and supply chain model. Police could be a problem.

My main competitor was Eddie, a friend of mine who retailed on the opposite corner. Eddie had a bad habit in that he liked to keep a lot of cash on hand. He was the kind of guy who got some satisfaction out of flashing his wad. He also had pockets full of change. Eddie was a walking cash register. I wasn't. I kept my cash hidden where I kept the fireworks. As things got noisy around our location with our customers anxious to demo the goods, I remember one occasion when the police showed up, and Eddie and I stood out—or maybe one of our customers fingered us. In a flash, they had us up against the wall and were into our pockets. I had a couple of coins, but Eddie was a walking branch bank. He got a ride to the station, and I resumed operations absent my competitor.

But can you imagine the Democrats presenting the image of me up against the wall being frisked at fifteen by the cops at my SCOTUS nomination hearings? That might be as bad as Kavanaugh's alleged high school sexual assaults. The only difference is mine would be based on facts.

By the way, Eddie was the son of the neighborhood doctor. He had three brothers, all of whom, including Eddie, became NYPD cadets straight out of high school and then became cops. Eddie retired from the police and, like so many of his fellows, passed away at a young age. At his wake, the neighborhood guys and I had fond reflections on our retail competition and Eddie's first ride in a cop car.

I learned some other things in my early retail operation that remained with me. At the start of the fireworks season, I didn't have much capital, and building inventory was a cash-and-carry operation. So, I had to borrow from friends to fund my initial operation. That came with a cost. In fact, I had to split my margin with my capital sources. So, a twenty-cent pack of firecrackers at retail meant a nickel profit for me and a nickel for my capital source. But the capital came with other benefits. The trip from the vacant lot to the subway could be a bit scary. Nothing ever happened, but I was always concerned about being relieved of my stock en route. Thinking back now, I suspect my Italian wholesalers must have had some kind of security in place. It would not have been good for business to have the supply chain interrupted so close to the source. But I was concerned, and fortunately, my sources of funding insisted on accompanying their capital to the point of purchase.

There goes any prospect of me getting a nomination to the bench! But I don't look good in black anyhow. Maybe a Federal Reserve nomination could be in the cards.

I had one other early retail operation, and it was in partnership with Eddie. His dad owned a bar with a back room for meetings and events. During high school and into college, we sold Christmas trees on the sidewalk outside the bar. Now get this. Every evening at the end of the workday, we stored the unsold trees in that back room. Do you have any idea what a fire hazard that was? We sure didn't, but we were just teens blinded by greed.

For every tree, there was a negotiation on both sides—both buying and selling. We bought the trees in bundles. Several trees were tied together and sold in lots of three to about six. The more in a bundle, the shorter the individual trees. But the most important factor was the branching. We had to learn to picture each tree by running our hand up the trunk, feeling for the branches on each tree in the bundle. If there were gaps where branches were missing, the tree would be more difficult to sell at full price. Depending on the condition of the trees, we'd offer a lower price than asked. Actually, we always offered a lower price.

Then there was the negotiation on the other side of the deal. Most of our customers were from the neighborhood, and some were family friends. No one wanted to pay the asking price, and that's when the haggling began. It all seemed par for the course after a while. And it was great training.

Italian Mary

My negotiating skills were honed most sharply in my dealings with Italian Mary. She was the lady who owned the local deli. As a youngster, my favorite food was a hero sandwich. That's the Italian sandwich on a roll that they call a sub, hoagie, or grinder, depending on where you live. Those were terms I learned only after leaving the Bronx. A hero at Italian Mary's was thirty-five cents, the price not negotiable. If you ever saw Italian Mary, you'd understand why haggling was out of the question. That was one large woman of commanding presence. But if the price was nonnegotiable, the ingredients were another matter. Buying a hero was a very personal encounter. You had to have your best game on. You see, Italian Mary hand-prepped every hero on the spot. She even sliced the meat and cheese special for each sandwich—none of that prepackaged-in-wax-paper, weighed stuff. Mary's heroes were custom deals made with Italian pride.

You never brought your boys when buying a hero. I knew instinctively that any expression of generosity on Italian Mary's part would be tempered in front of potentially additional sales. So, there I was on one side of the counter and Italian Mary and her slicer on the other. Big smile, lots of "pleases," and an occasional "Yes, ma'am, I really like your Italian salami a lot." It was clear I wasn't Italian, so it always helped to show some sensitivity over that ethnic divide. Anything to get an extra slice. The more I talked and smiled, the more Italian Mary sliced. That thirty-five cents had to get as much hero as possible. That's where the negotiating skills originated—on the customer side of the counter at Italian Mary's. Tasty memories.

Today I go to Firehouse Subs. Founded by a couple of Jacksonville, Florida, firefighter brothers. Great sandwich and I get loyalty points for each purchase, but it ain't Italian Mary's, and it's all premeasured. There's no room to negotiate, no opportunity to schmooze. I miss you, Italian Mary. Thanks for all those extra slices. Most of all, thanks for those life lessons.

Working Down Under

During college, I worked for about a year in the New York City subways painting the Grand Central shuttle station. The 42nd Street Shuttle is the shortest line in the subway system running below 42nd Street between the Times Square and Grand Central stations. There had been a fire at the Grand Central station requiring extensive replacement of steel components and subsequent painting. The restoration work had to be done at night because they kept the shuttle running at least part of the time. I worked from about 11:00 p.m. to 6:00 a.m. as an apprentice painter earning time and a half. I remember that my base pay, which was $3.50 per hour, increased to $5.25 for night work.

I went directly from the job to college classes at 242nd Street and Broadway. We used oil-based paint, and the only way I had to clean myself up was by using kerosene. Between that and the lead-based paint I scraped off the platforms without even a mask, I probably lost about thirty points on my IQ. Where was OSHA when I really needed them? But $5.25 was a lot, and that summer, I went on to paint bridges around the city when not working in the ballparks. There weren't that many people who wanted to sit near me in class. But then, none of them were making $5.25 an hour either.

The subway work was priced on a time and materials basis. That meant the contractor passed on the costs to the city. It was union work, and the union assigned its older and disabled members, along with the most inexperienced like me, to the time and materials jobs. One of my jobs was to assist the master union members. That meant I schlepped their paint, laid out drop cloths, and helped them "walk" their ladders. Walking was the process of moving the ladder as the painter progressed in painting the steel girders above. Walking meant we could move the ladder without the painter coming down.

As I remember, I was the only native-born American on the job and the only guy with English as a first language. I had plenty of high school and college Spanish, French, and Latin but lots of luck using any of that with these guys. Most of the older guys were Italian, Greek, or Polish, and they all chewed tobacco.

My fondest memory of helping one of my senior fellows was working with Valentino. I don't know whether that was his first name or his last name. He was just Valentino. As near as I could tell, Valentino spoke no English. In fact, I don't think Valentino spoke. He just grunted—and spat tobacco juice. A lot of that tobacco juice landed on me. Did I mention the $5.25 per hour? As Valentino completed a section, I grabbed the ladder, and we started walking it with Valentino topside and me down below. For reasons still unknown to me, the walking process involved an acceleration in Valentino's expectorating. With each hit, I yelled out, "Valentino, you son of a bitch!" It seemed to me that only helped him keep score of his hits. I just found it tough to respect my elder fellow worker when he was spitting on me.

Mom and Pop, the Best Parents Ever

My parents were both originally from an area in the southeast sector of Ireland, County Wicklow. They came by ship, my father from Liverpool, England, where he'd been a ship's carpenter, and my mother from Dublin. My father had served an apprenticeship in an Irish shipyard in Arklow. He was pretty much an indentured servant there and then moved to Liverpool once he got his master's certification. My parents didn't know each other before they came to America and met in New York City.

Back then, immigrants had to be "claimed." That meant someone had to vouch for them in the event they failed to properly support themselves. The same couple, Mick and Nellie Byrne, vouched for both Mom and Pop. My mother found a job working in a hotel in Connecticut, and my father got a job with the Independent Rail

Transit System, or the IRT, in the city. The IRT was one of the predecessor private rail components to the NYC public rail transit system.

What most folks don't know is that New York City did not build the original subway system. It was a consolidation of several privately developed and owned rail lines. That's where the acronyms for the various lines come from, the IRT, the BMT, and the IND. They were the names of the original private rail lines. A great book about the development and evolution of the NYC subway system is *Uptown, Downtown: A Trip Through Time on New York's Subways* by Stan Fischler. A terrific book.

My parents arrived during the Great Depression. The Depression was the one time in US history that more people emigrated from the country than immigrated here. I like to think Mom and Pop made the great contrarian investment. That is, they went short on the old country and long on the US when most were going the other way. That was a great market call because the US has prospered greatly since the Depression, and their family, in particular, has done terrific here.

Between my fourth and fifth grades, my mother, father, younger brother, and I traveled to Ireland for a couple of weeks. We stayed on the farm where my mother grew up, which was run by my Uncle Paddy, my mother's oldest surviving brother. Paddy was a guy who had migrated to the US and returned as the oldest son to run the farm when his parents became disabled. Having spent my entire life in New York City, I wasn't prepared for how green and beautiful Ireland was. But what struck me the most was how different the people were from those I knew back in the Bronx. In the Bronx, Irish immigrants had multiple jobs, and everyone was constantly hustling. On the farm in Ireland, there seemed to be a lot of tea drinking and smoking out in the yard. The two people working hardest on the farm were Mom and Pop. The farmhouse had no running water or electricity. There were no toilets, the kitchen had a dirt floor, and they cooked over the fireplace. Over the years and on multiple trips, my mother would change all that. She looked and sounded like everyone else on the farm, but the neighbors came to refer to her and my father as "the Americans."

I came to understand American exceptionalism at an early age. I didn't know it then, but as supers in the Bronx, we were pretty close to the lowest rung on the American economic ladder. I remember sitting in the kitchen of my mother's family farmhouse on that first trip to the old country. We were all sitting in a circle and talking.

I remember whispering, "Mom, I need to go to the bathroom."

She responded, "Just go outside."

I figured she meant there was some kind of outhouse. I wandered around and found nothing, then went back to my mother's side and said, "Mom, I can't find the toilet."

"Go out in the field and pick a spot," she answered.

Talk about culture shock!

Here's my other vivid memory. We were in Ireland during the fall blackberry season. Each room had a chamber pot for nighttime ablutions. That took some getting used to for a youngster from the Bronx. The farm was segmented into sections, the borders of which were what they called stone "ditches." That is, the stones from clearing the fields had been used to create borders for the field. Blackberry bushes grew out of those stone borders, and in the fall of each year, the farmers harvested the berries. My family was pressed into the blackberry harvest, and when I questioned the hygienic implications of using chamber pots for collecting the blackberries, my Mom said, "Don't worry, these blackberries are for export to the English." An interesting lesson in the geopolitics of Ireland and England.

In time, I came to believe that not all Americans are born in America. Many are born someplace else and must find their way home. Later, I would hear the expression, "The ones with the get up and go got up and went." That's the way I came to see immigration and certainly the way I came to think of Mom and Pop. That guy who schleps his three-year-old from Honduras to Texas was born an American. He just happened to be born in Honduras. We have to find the right way to get them here legally.

My parents may never have bought a stock, but they made that one great trade from which their entire family has benefitted. They went long on the US and short on Europe at precisely the right time. Thanks, Mom and Pop, great market call!

The Founders of the MYFR System

Mom and Pop were tough, hardworking people who were strongly committed to the education and prosperity of their children. They never owned a business or a stock, and until late in life, they never owned real estate or a car. But they raised four successful, well-educated, and prosperous children. They were the founders of the Make Your Family Rich system. The three sons, me included, all earned advanced degrees from prominent universities. Mike earned a Ph.D. in chemistry from Purdue University, John an MBA from Fordham University, and I earned a law degree from Georgetown University Law Center. John and I both earned our advanced degrees after marrying by attending night school.

It all worked out great for us, but it all started with Mom and Pop, their example, their work and energy, and their powerful values. Oh, and those great charter schools. That's how I think now about those urban Catholic schools we attended. They were the early charters; they were great schools, and the teachers were superb.

Years later, I would see a bumper sticker that said, "I survived Catholic schools." There's some truth there, but what a fabulous education in one of the poorest neighborhoods in the country. I didn't know we were in the poor section at the time, and it would have made no difference. But it's relevant today when poverty seems to be considered a handicap and blamed for all kinds of problems, such as low expectations and underperformance. In our country, I don't see being born poor as a handicap. The tools and opportunities were there for me and my brothers and sister. Our parents were terrific in making sure we were encouraged to seize every opportunity and had the incentive to perform and advance. My mother and father were the founders of the Make Your Family Rich system. I have modernized and securitized things, but the foundational values are the same as those transmitted to me.

Separating Earning a Living from Investing

I would go on to have lots of jobs in different fields. I would also invest in many ways, particularly in real estate. It would take me quite some time to fully isolate the role of an investor from that of an employee and business owner. At first, it was all about making money in whatever legal way earned the most—except for that fireworks stint. But this book is about being an investor in the securities market. It's about isolating the investor role from all the other roles involved in generating income or cash flow. I believe focusing as early as possible on being an investor in the US securities market using the MYFR system is the most efficient way to achieve great wealth over time. That's the story of creating and living the FINER life.

I went on too long about my background and origins. But it may be important. With all the immigrants coming into the country, there's a reason they want to be here, and perhaps my family's story offers an explanation about why they come. I know that if I was born someplace else, I'd beat a path to the US lickety-split. I'd like to think I'd get my forms in order first.

4

INVEST ONLY IN DIVIDEND CHAMPIONS

T HE FIRST PRINCIPLE OF THE MYFR SYSTEM IS to measure your success and the performance of your asset management business by your *income* rather than *the value* of your business, which fluctuates with the vagaries of the market. Rarely will a professional financial advisor adhere to any performance measure other than the value of your portfolio. But think about that for a bit. You have no control over what the market does. Markets fluctuate for an infinite number of reasons, none of which you can affect. I always remember the quote of noted investment manager John Templeton about the performance of markets: "Bull markets are born on pessimism, grow on skepticism, mature on optimism, and die on euphoria." That's been my observation of market patterns. If you believe that, then the best investment advisor would be a market shrink who understands the psychology of the public and investors.

The professional investment manager will tell you he or she has some special expertise or that they have access to experts who've been successful in picking individual stocks. A professional investor typically has to get it right on each stock at least twice. That is, they need to pick the right time to buy, and then they also must determine the best point to sell. You probably get the same emails I do that tout guys who picked the last market collapse or recommended Apple when it was $10. If you have the patience to listen to their entire spiel, you'll eventually get the sales pitch to buy a particular fund, sign up with an advisor, or buy his or her newsletter.

The Business Cycle

Depicted in the following chart is a dramatization of the US business cycle over some hypothetical period. During my lifetime, the business cycle has been a series of repeating sine curves (to use a technical term). The ups and downs are much more irregular or squiggly than the very smooth curves in the chart, but generally, the pattern is that equity values increase during times of economic expansion and contract in recessionary periods. You or your financial advisor may be able to pick the general trend of the economy, and that's important. But will you or they be able to pick the individual stocks that do best in both expansions and recessions?

THE BUSINESS CYCLE

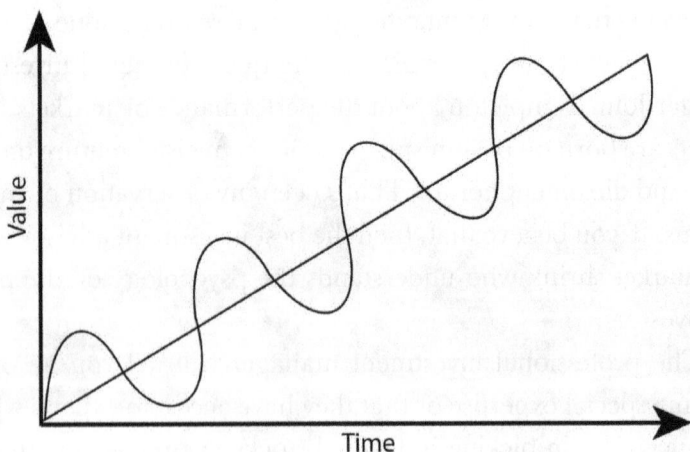

The positively sloping straight line is another dramatization. We use it to depict the constantly increasing dividend income generated by dividend-growth stocks. We recommend a particular class of dividend growth businesses, but that part of the graph you *can* control by limiting yourself to businesses with constantly increasing dividends. This business cycle graph will be important in our further discussion of the MYFR system. Do you think it would look good on an MYFR T-shirt? Another view of the positively sloping line is of the general direction of the market over time. That is, if your horizon is long enough, the equity markets will ascend to higher highs and descend to higher lows. That's been the pattern over my lifetime.

What's a Dividend Champion?

The key concept of the Make Your Family Rich system is to invest only in Dividend Champions. At this writing, Dividend Champions are the 143 almost exclusively American-based public businesses that have paid their owners an increasing dividend for at least twenty-five years. Dividends, of course, are the regular payments, usually paid quarterly, that are made to the owners of a public company. It's quite an accomplishment to pay dividends for twenty-five or more years. It's even more significant and admirable to pay an increasing dividend over that many years. The last twenty-five years have seen three recessions, and during each of those periods, the Dividend Champions continued to pay increasing distributions. Now that's performance and commitment.

You often hear about moats from folks involved in securities analysis. *Moat* is a term used to describe the protection afforded a business that has high barriers to entry for competitors. Take a business that owns several patents as an example. A pharmaceutical firm with a patent on a particularly effective drug for a common disease might be said to have a wide and deep moat around their business—at least for the duration of the patent. Similarly, for a business that is very capital intensive, it might also be difficult to create an alternative to compete with the existing business. You could think of the moat as being the basis for the monopoly-like business of the moat-protected company.

I like to think of long-term increasing dividends as a moat. Think about the Dividend Champion company. You come along as the new CEO, and on your way to your new office, you pass down a hall with the portraits of your predecessors, all of whom have sustained the culture of rewarding the company's owners with constantly increasing dividends. Do you want to be the guy or gal who breaks that tradition? Are you going to be the guy who de-Dividend Champions the company? Or are you going to move mountains and anything else in the way that impedes you from increasing the company's earnings to give your owners a raise? That's called CEO moat motivation.

Going into the COVID collapse in the spring of 2020, there were 140 Dividend Champions. With a 35% decline in the market value, only two Dividend Champions stopped increasing their dividends. They were Ross Stores (ROST), a retail operation, and Helmerich and Payne (HP), a contract energy driller. At the time, ROST had increased dividends for twenty-seven years and HP for forty-seven years. We owned both companies and promptly started selling call options, and we eventually sold our interest in the two businesses.

In 2020, the *Wall Street Journal* reported that nearly 190 US-listed companies stopped paying dividends. Thirty-nine resumed paying dividends that same year, fifty-three followed suit in 2021, and twenty-three restarted by the fall of 2022, with 38.5% yet to reinstate their distributions. Even in the face of such an enormous market drop and economic disruption, 138 of the 140 Dividend Champions not only continued their dividends but also increased their payouts. Now that's the stuff of a true Champion. Can you see Rocky up there at the top of the steps, arms raised? Yeah!

There are about 7,000 US public companies and 60,000 worldwide. At least with respect to US-listed companies, there is a mountain of data on each. Get on any financial or stock brokerage site, enter the ticker symbol for a stock, and you can unlock virtually unlimited information on that business's past and current performance. There are annual and quarterly reports, Securities and Exchange Commission filings, endless press releases and news reports, and all sorts of comparisons with competitors and other stocks.

You could make a career out of becoming proficient in the leading companies in a single industry. In fact, people make a career out of doing just that, and you constantly see them on CNBC and Bloomberg. Or you can subscribe to analysts' newsletters or watch their podcasts. Then what do you do? You decide in which stocks you'll invest your family's money. Then what do you do? You stay wired into these guys and their publications to decide when to sell those stocks. After all, if these folks are smart enough to tell you what and when to buy, they must be smart enough to know when you should sell, right? I get an Excedrin headache just thinking about all those investment options and the tons of data and opinions involved.

Look, all those really smart financial folks feel your pain. That's what their business is—feeling and relieving your pain. They do that in one of two main ways. Either they become your financial advisor and guide you in the selection of the businesses they believe will be uniquely successful. They level those mountains of data on the way to designing your very special investment portfolio for a fee. That's one way. The other way is they become mutual fund or ETF managers. Mutual funds are aggregations of stocks based on a particular theme, like global growth investing or groupings intended to match the performance of a variety of market indices. Mutual funds tend to be actively managed with restrictions on the timing of trading. Management fees for mutual funds are higher than ETFs. An Exchange Traded Fund also represents a portfolio of stocks, but as the name implies, they are traded on the exchanges very much like stocks. ETFs tend to be more passively managed, designed to track a particular index, and, therefore, have lower management fees.

Warren Buffett frequently says that most investors would be best off simply buying index funds and holding them forever. In a way, Buffett is validating the business cycle chart we depicted earlier in this chapter. Another way of looking at the investment options is that any person, over time, is unlikely to be more successful picking individual stocks than by simply investing in the long-term direction of markets. That's pretty much what Mr. Buffett believes and often says.

Let Mrs. Market Select the Businesses

At this point, it's good to emphasize again that the first principle of the Make Your Family Rich system is to *measure success by the income generated by the business*, not the market's view of the value of said businesses. We cannot control the market's valuation. We can control our income. We control our income by investing only in Dividend Champions.

I always come back to the difference between owning a business and owning stocks. My earliest experience was all about owning a business, and my focus was on how much money I generated in a given time period. My analogy is owning that big Italian restaurant. OK, my origins are Irish, but there are very few, if any, Irish restaurants. Who in their right mind opens an Irish restaurant? Our family could have developed a large Italian restaurant, and our focus would be today's sales. Why? Because that would mostly determine the success of our business and the prosperity of our family. The value of our real estate and the food service business might fluctuate over time, but the one certainty is the number of sales and the money in the cash register each day.

We emphasize that owning only Dividend Champions is about owning an interest in great American businesses. The daily, hourly, or even momentary fluctuation in the value of the stock of that business is just a distraction. It's the market's derived value of our business. The current price is where millions of buyers and sellers can agree on a price in the massive dynamic auction that is the various stock markets around the world. The determination of market value is based on millions of people's feelings at any given time. The variables that the trading millions consider in making pricing decisions are infinite. It's about who in the world is shooting at whom or who they are threatening to shoot at. It's about what various central banks are talking about. Elections around the world can affect values. Takeovers of one company by another can influence the direction of market values. How about folks' view of when the next recession starts, or are we already in a recession, or maybe Europe is entering a recession? Just tune in to CNBC or Bloomberg and listen to the talking heads, and someone will tell you why markets and individual industries and stocks are up or down. Then the next guy will give you his confident but contrary view.

Fuhgeddaboudit! Listen to Mrs. Market. Hear her? She's telling you to check the cash register. That will tell you how your business is really performing. Your business is the family's asset management business, which is the wide variety of great income-producing businesses you own. Every day the cash register at Mrs. Market's store shows more money. Skeptical? Count it. You see, your brokerage statement will show your estimated annual income is up month to month. But you really know it's increasing daily, and it takes a month to confirm that.

Ignore Market Fluctuations

Yeah, right! That will never happen. Look, as I write this, the Dow is down 738 points. That's a day after the Federal Reserve Bank raised the rate by seventy-five basis points. The market rallied about 300 points when the rate was increased. The three trading days before the rate increase, the Dow dropped almost 2,000 points. Were those dramatic market fluctuations caused by the anticipation and/or the reality of the Fed's actions? Who knows. Even if you are a committed Make Your Family Rich business owner, there never will be a day when those kinds of market drops won't cause anxiety. They will. But that's not important.

What's important is not how you feel; it's what you do. Go back and look at that business cycle chart at the beginning of this chapter. The market value always comes back and eventually to new highs. But while you're waiting, your income keeps increasing as long as you're invested in those great Dividend Champions.

Also, make sure to focus on Chapter 7, "How to Control the Gnu in You." If you can control the gnu in you, you'll avoid selling your businesses when the market sustains a significant decline. Remember, it's not about how you feel in a down market. You'll never feel good. It's what you do that matters. By focusing on your constantly increasing income, you'll be much less inclined to sell.

Accessing the Dividend Champions Data

On the first of every month, we get our Dividend Champion list and a mountain of data on each business from Wide Moat Research (www.widemoatresearch.com). The list and data were originally developed and maintained by David Fish starting in 2007. David made the data available for free to his fans on Seeking Alpha (www.seekingalpha.com). That's where I first found David. It's a huge amount of data, and we've been using it for years. David passed in 2019, and Justin Law picked up the baton and now offers the information on Wide Moat Research. On the first day or two of each month, Justin distributes new data. He also periodically issues a report that highlights one of the individual stocks.

Justin's list is not limited to the Dividend Champions. He also maintains separate listings on *Dividend Contenders* that have increasing dividends for between ten and twenty-four years. Finally, he provides the same data for *Dividend Challengers*, where dividends have increased from five to nine years. Justin also compiles a single CCC list where he combines the Champions, Contenders, and Challenges. At the beginning of each month, I save the lists and print the Dividend Champions and the CCC lists. I keep the two printed lists in a three-ring binder and replace them when Justin distributes the new data each month.

Justin distributes the data in two ways: as a PDF file and as a standard spreadsheet. There are lots of columns in the spreadsheet, and I find it helpful to delete the columns I don't use. Inevitably, you'll want to concentrate on certain data elements. For example, I concentrate on the number of years that dividends have increased and the current dividend amount and rate. Also, the rate of dividend increase over the last year or two and the average annual rate of increase for the last ten years is particularly important to me. A higher annual rate of increase indicates that the business managers have confidence in their continuing ability to provide increasing dividends. Justin's spreadsheet has a wealth of information on each business and even includes the number of recessions during which the company paid increasing dividends.

What We Do with the Dividend Champion List

We'll fully describe how we use Justin's lists in our daily trading in the next chapter. You may struggle through that chapter at first. Man, will it be worth it! It's one of my favorite topics and chapters. Once you understand the technique, you'll love it. Then you'll wonder why everyone doesn't embrace the technique.

Are There Exceptions?

Sure. There are exceptions for us to the *Invest Only in Dividend Champions* rule. I suspect, over time, there will be for you, too. We will go over our exceptions logic in Chapter 6, "Scratch the Itch But Not a Lot."

5

SELL THE DIPS; OUT-OF-THE-MONEY *PUT OPTIONS*, THAT IS

I'VE BEEN ATTENDING THE REGULAR MEETINGS of a local investing group for a couple of months now. At those meetings, I've introduced the notion of selling out-of-the-money *puts* as a better way to buy equities and increase income. I would characterize the investing group's method of selecting stocks as *fundamental analysis*. They try to do all those things the financial advisor folks on CNBC do by evaluating the fundamentals of various businesses to find undervalued stocks or ones with superior growth potential. You know the approach. It's the one with all the graphs and charts in search of that special insight to select an underpriced stock.

When I introduced the idea of selling *put* options, the reception from my fellow investors was skeptical. That's generous. I get that reaction a lot. Many people understand the mathematics of selling puts but can't bring themselves to execute a trade. I think that inaction has a lot to do with the language involved in trading options. I hate to say it, but the older the investor, the more reluctant they seem to be to consider the opportunity. Often, too, the options skeptic thinks that selling options must involve the risk of incurring debt. It doesn't. That's a choice you can make, and I'll explain the risks and potential rewards of debt.

There are many well-founded fears about trading options. Years ago, as I first introduced my children to the details of how their family asset management business was run, including the sale of put options, my son Matt expressed reservations.

"Dad, it seems that many stories I've read about investors going broke involve trading in options."

Today, Matt and his sister Erin manage that asset management business, and most days, they sell put options. In fact, they keep a diary of their transactions on our website (www.makeyourfamilyrich. com). I think now, with the benefit of experience, they see selling put options as a more lucrative way of buying the businesses we want to own. It really need not be more complicated than that; selling puts is just a better way to buy most businesses, and that's true whether you employ the MYFR system or have another approach to selecting your investments.

As mentioned before, our Make Your Family Rich system involves investing almost exclusively in Dividend Champions, which are the 143 or so mostly domestic, publicly traded businesses that have increased their dividends for at least twenty-five years. These are the great, largely American businesses like MCD, KO, MMM, PG, CL, JNJ, WMT, and many others we all know and patronize. We think their common dividend persistence provides a wide and deep moat around the value of the businesses.

Sell the Dips

It's how we pursue the opportunity to buy the Dividend Champions that's the key to this chapter. We rarely directly buy the businesses we target for acquisition. You see, we "Sell the Dips." Selling the dips is when one of the Dividend Champions declines a significant amount on any trading day. We typically sell cash-backed, out-of-the-money puts. What that means is that on a day when a Dividend Champion may drop, say 3% to 5%, when others are buying the dip, we sell a put option, usually at least 10% to 15% below the dipped price— with an expiration date no more than ninety days in the future.

That may seem a bit complicated. Let me give a basic example of how it works. Let's say a particular Dividend Champion we like has been selling for $100. On a day when the market experiences a down draft, that stock may drop to $96, at which time we might sell a put with a strike price of $85, expiring on a date three months hence. That means that if, on the expiration date, the stock is below $85, we are committed to paying the owner $85 to buy the stock. By the way, "out-of-the-money" simply means below the current price. So, selling an $85 put when the market price is $96 is selling an out-of-the-money put.

Here's an interesting way to look at selling out-of-the-money puts. Selling out-of-the-money puts is effectively operating a side insurance gig. By selling the put, we guarantee the current owner of the stock that on a day when his or her confidence might be a bit shaken because the stock is down a lot, if the stock continues to decline, they'll be protected from an even larger and perhaps catastrophic loss. For committing to that obligation, we receive an insurance premium which is the *put* sales price. In this case, depending on the underlying stock and the volume of options trading, the premium might be about $2.50 a share. Because options trade on the basis of contracts consisting of 100 shares, the premium paid would be $250 per contract, less whatever modest commission the broker charges. In our case, the broker's fee is sixty-five cents. That net premium is then instantly deposited to the put seller's account. If, on the expiration date, the put holder must buy the shares at $85, the net cost is actually $82.50 (the price of $85, less the put premium of $2.50 previously paid).

What's not to like? On a trading day when the business you want to own dips a lot, you (the put seller) receive $250 to guarantee the stock owner that you'll buy the business interest if the price declines another 10% or so. We think of that as our great side insurance gig. Beats the heck out of being an Uber driver!

To identify sell-the-dip opportunities, we maintain a spreadsheet of all Dividend Champions on Yahoo Finance. We custom design our Yahoo spreadsheet to include only the factors we consider most relevant. Each month we update our Yahoo Finance spreadsheet to reflect any change in the Dividend Champions. Usually, there are no changes, but occasionally one will be added. Less frequently, a Dividend Champion fails to increase its dividend and will be dropped from the list by Justin Law. Appendix A has an excerpt from our Yahoo worksheet. Simply by clicking on the %Change column, the list of Dividend Champions will be ordered based on the greatest declining Dividend Champions. We tend to prefer the business that, at the time of our search, has declined the most, but we'll also consider how much of that business we already own. We determine whether options are available on the individual business and how liquid the options market is for that business. All but a few of the Dividend Champions offer options, and the ones that don't tend to be the smaller businesses. Conversely, the larger the business, the more liquid both its stock and the options are. By liquid, we mean that there's substantial trading at any given time in the issues. That also means that the spread between the bid and ask prices on both the stock and options are tighter. The tighter the spread, the more likely you can comfortably enter a market order on the put sale. That's like the bid-and-ask dynamic when buying stock directly.

More on How Puts Work

We never, ever sell a put on a business we don't want to own. Most puts we sell never execute. That means we don't buy the underlying stock. If they do execute, we're happy to buy at the lower net price. If the stock does not execute, we are also happy because we have made a nice return on our cash. Let's explain that last point. Selling a cash-backed put means that we have the cash available to buy the stock, and if the price is below our strike price on the execution date, we will buy the stock.

In our earlier case, we received $250 for reserving $8,500 ($85 x 100 shares) for three months. That's a 2.9% return for the three-month term or 11.8% annualized. That's about the range we're experiencing in Matt and Erin's recent trades. Check their trading diary on www.makeyourfamilyrich.com for specific transactions, where they also compute the cash-on-cash returns on each put sale.

Mrs. Market does not give us many win-win deals, but we think selling cash-backed, short-term, out-of-the-money puts on dips in the stocks we want to own is just such a deal. That's a mouthful, but any deal this good is worth learning and gaining a command of the options vocabulary.

Why doesn't everyone sell cash-backed, short-term, out-of-the-money puts on stocks they want to own? I've frequently been asked that. Well, not exactly in those words, but I'm asked, "If this is such a good idea, why isn't everyone doing it?" I think it's mostly about the *vocabulary* of options. Standard stock investors need to learn a new vocabulary. They are not *buying* a stock; they are *selling* a put. The prospective stock investor isn't bidding on a purchase price but bidding on an option's premium or put sales price. It's about *out-of-the-money*—and would you believe you can sell *at the money* or *in the money*? Like all new languages, it takes some practice.

A headline in the September 26, 2022, *Wall Street Journal* caught my eye: "Stock Downturn Brings Pain to Buy-the-Dip Investors." The article noted that during the mostly down market in 2022, many buy-the-dip investors were feeling pain. They bought the dip, and their stocks kept going down. I understand that. In our case, we've generally been selling puts on down days and on the Dividend Champions that have declined the most. Then, we're selling the dip in this market at strike prices about 15% lower.

Does that guarantee you caught the bottom? Of course not. But if the Dividend Champion continues to decline, you'll buy it at an additional 15% lower. If the Dividend Champion bounces back or doesn't decline the full 15% by the expiration date, you keep the premium. Anything there you don't like, you disgruntled buy-the-dip investor? It's a Mrs. Market win-win deal. What a neat lady!

Time Arbitrage

Time arbitrage—that's what Steve Sears calls the selling of out-of-the-money puts on stocks you want to own long term. Steve writes the "Striking Point" column weekly for *Barron's*. It's one of the first things I read on Saturday morning. I think you should, too. Time arbitrage, he says in his October 24, 2022, column "Things Could Get Worse, You Need a Better Strategy," is the "strategy that seeks to balance the risks of today"—of which he thinks there are many—"with the potential rewards of tomorrow." That's what we're doing. For the option premium, we take advantage of opportunities in a down market or with particular Dividend Champions to commit to buying at even lower prices. We do that because, in the longer term, which for us is forever, we believe the current pricing will be a good deal.

Remember the Business Cycle chart from Chapter 4? It showed that over time, market values ascend to new highs. It's nice having a fancy name like *time arbitrage* to describe this aspect of the Make Your Family Rich system. Thanks, Steve, and I'll see you on Saturday.

Margin Backed Put Selling

Look, options have a spotty reputation, and much of that is deserved. Options can be misused, and the temptation to do so can be great. Taking a simple example, the reader will remember the put premium is received upon acceptance of the offer to sell the put. Let's say the put sale is not backed by cash but by the investor's available margin. That means the put seller doesn't have the cash available to cover the possible purchase. In that case, if the option expires unexecuted, then the investor's return is infinite. The return is infinite because the debt will only be incurred if the option executes, and if the option expires unexecuted, the debt is never incurred. Then the numerator in the return-on-investment equation is the premium, and the denominator—or the cash invested—is zero. In that case, the put seller's return is infinite. Returns don't get better than infinite.

The temptation, then, is to sell options on margin. The use of margin is tempting in stock investing, too. That is, if you really believe a stock is going higher, you potentially maximize your return by buying that stock on margin because you expect the return to be greater than the cost of the borrowed funds. Just like you should avoid buying stock on margin, you should not use margin to sell puts. If you do sell puts on margin, please do it in moderation.

What does our put selling mean for us in our returns? An account statement in the spring of 2022 estimated our annual dividend return on the businesses we own is 2.2%. I occasionally maintain a worksheet of our options premiums from which I project an annualized return, which I estimated then at about 2.7% of the portfolio value. We had recently sold a lot of real estate and were holding more cash than usual, so those returns may not be normal. Suffice it to say the selling-the-dip options method we use to buy the businesses we target for acquisition is the source of some significant supplemental income.

During the summer of 2022 and at the time of this writing, things changed. The country is facing a recession, and the market is down almost 20% since the beginning of the year. We've been buying additional shares over the last year because we've generated cash from real estate sales. We still have cash, but not as much as we had eight months ago. Most of our purchases have resulted from the market decline as some of our options have executed, and we've bought stock. That's a good thing. It's never a bad time to buy Dividend Champions or sell out-of-the-money put options on Dividend Champions.

Our Use of Debt

We do run the risk of incurring debt in put selling on Dividend Champions. By that, I mean that Matt and Erin maintain a worksheet that keeps track of the amount of debt should all our puts result in purchases. The three of us agree on the maximum amount of potential debt. With our generally negative view of current market prospects, we're now limiting the potential margin to 10% of the total equity value of our asset management business. That's also a function of our estimate of the capital that could be made available from other assets. With our real estate holdings reduced, we have limited additional capital from that source. Plus, in a general market decline like we experienced at the end of 2022, incurring debt should be strictly curtailed if not avoided entirely. We have negotiated a very favorable margin rate, but with rising interest rates and declining markets, it's time to limit potential debt.

If, in a steep down market, you find yourself potentially incurring too much margin debt, you can always *"buy to cancel"* your put options. Typically, such action will result in a loss, but usually, the loss will be significantly less than if you had bought the stock. "Buy to cancel"—now there's some more options lingo for you.

6

SCRATCH THE ITCH
BUT NOT A LOT

THE MYFR SYSTEM CAN SEEM A BIT ROBOTIC. Limiting yourself to the 143 Dividend Champions from time to time might feel restraining. That's natural. You may think you have a special understanding of a particular company or industry. That, you think, will give you an investing edge. Variants from the MYFR system of investing in Dividend Champions we call *Scratch the Itch (STI) investments*. We think if you have that itch, it's okay to scratch it, but we suggest you do it in moderation. Look, I like the kind of robotics that gives us a constantly increasing income. But I understand that with all the financial news and analyses out there, some folks think they have a special insight and are just plain smarter than the market. It's simply human nature, and if you don't scratch, that itch might drive you crazy.

Our STIs

Our STIs fall into two categories. First, we own a lot of Washington, DC, area community banks. The DC metro area is an extremely affluent community, and we lived there for several years. From an early age, I was an active real estate investor and needed a ready source of mortgage financing. When I started in my early twenties, I had very little capital and knew I needed strong banking relationships. With what little money I had, I bought an interest in a local community bank. I became friendly with the principals in the bank, particularly the lending officers. I also made it a habit to attend the bank's annual meetings. They usually provided snacks, and after the formal presentation, there were drinks and an opportunity to interact with the bank officials and the few community bank analysts who attended. Very few stockholders took the trouble to attend the meetings, and I gradually got to know everyone and developed an understanding of the individual bank and the local banking industry. I also tried to attend the quarterly earnings calls if the bank held them.

As the years passed and I continued to accumulate real estate and capital, I diversified into a number of local community banks. I always found it advantageous to have a relationship and own an interest in at least two or three local banks. I didn't hesitate to let one bank know I was also talking with another local bank when I applied for financing. No bank official will ever say that you get better terms as a stockholder, but I do believe you get some preference in terms and processing as an owner. Besides, who wants to be the loan officer who turns down a loan to that nice stockholder who always shows up at the annual meetings and earnings calls?

After a couple of years, I noticed a pattern. There tended to be an incubation period for new community banks during which they grew rapidly, and eventually, they were either bought by or merged into a larger bank. When that happened, we experienced a nice pop in the value of our interest. Year after year, there were more new or *de novo* community banks as older ones were sold or merged. As banks were sold or merged, we bought into the new up-and-comers, and I always went to the annual meetings and sat in on the quarterly earnings calls.

As I look at our most recent experience, none of the Washington, DC, community banks we owned eight years ago still exists in their original form. They've all been bought or merged into a larger local or regional bank. We always made a nice return on the acquisition.

Over time, I found that I made more money on my bank investments than I did on the real estate I bought with the banks' mortgage financing. That takes more explanation. You see, my community bank acquisitions involved little or no work on my part. Sure, I attended some meetings and spent some time analyzing financials and the like, but I was almost purely an investor in the banks' securities. Contrast that to my real estate *investing*, where I was a jack-of-all-trades who negotiated leases, maintained properties, arranged repairs, dealt with tenants and partners—and a whole lot more. In effect, I was primarily running a real estate business and was somewhat coincidentally an investor. In the case of my local community bank holdings, I was almost exclusively an investor. The business owner vs. investor roles became an important distinction that came into sharper focus as I developed the Make Your Family Rich system.

Our most recent DC community bank acquisition is Trustar Bank. One of almost twenty *de novo* banks in 2019, we bought into a small interest in the initial private offering. We'd been investors in Washington First Bank, which had sold to Sandy Spring Bank (SASR), and the principals in Washington First had taken leadership positions in Sandy Spring. In situations like that, the principals in the merged bank normally agree that they won't initiate a new bank for a set time after the acquisition. When that time had elapsed, the Washington First alumni launched the new bank, Trustar. Trustar has been the fastest-growing bank among the 2019 class of *de novo* banks. When Trustar offered us the opportunity to buy an additional interest in a secondary private offering in 2022, we bought an additional modest interest. Although we believe Trustar is a wonderful investment opportunity, we haven't bought a more substantial interest because we don't expect Trustar to pay a dividend any time soon. You know how much we covet those growing dividends! Moreover, we've reduced our real estate ownership in the Washington, DC, area and don't foresee a need for local mortgage financing. That said, a couple of years ago, we originated a residential mortgage with Trustar, and it was a very positive, professional experience. Due to the pandemic, Trustar did not have an annual in-person meeting until the spring of 2023, which I attended. Community banks have been struggling since the failure of Silicon Valley Bank. The presentations by Trustar leadership were all positive. They also honored John Dalton, the former Secretary of the Navy, who they announced was retiring as a bank director to become director emeritus. Oh, and the few stockholders attending each received an autographed copy of John's new book, *At the Helm*—great guy, a great book, and a great annual meeting. Sometimes those STIs can be very rewarding.

This category of STI is likely to continue to decline with time. As a rough rule, we are no longer acquiring real estate, and that includes in the Washington, DC, area. So that additional incentive to acquire DC community banks no longer exists. We'll probably make an exception with Trustar but are not inclined to buy a lot of the bank—at least not before it starts paying a dividend.

Tech Dividend Champion Wannabes

Our other STI category is tech businesses. Of the current 143 Dividend Champions, only five are classified as being in the information technology industry. That's not a lot, but the limited number makes sense. Information technology is one of the newer, high-growth industries. Typically, high-growth firms tend to reinvest their earnings to fund research and development and additional growth. They seem to have particularly robust rates at which they raise their annual dividends. The names of the five businesses currently on Justin Law's Dividend Champions list, their trading symbol, the number of years they've increased dividends to July 2022, and the average annual rate of dividend increase are as follows:

Trading Symbol	Name	# Years	Annual Rate
ADP	Automatic Data Processing Inc.	46	11.5%
BMI	Badger Meters Inc.	29	9.7%
CSVI	Computer Services Inc.	50	16.0%
IBM	International Business Machines Inc.	27	8.5%
JCHY	Jake Henry and Associates Inc.	47	15.9%

If you worked for one of these companies and got that kind of salary increase through good times and bad, you might be reasonably satisfied and inclined to stick with the company. We think it should be the same with owners.

With the exception of IBM and maybe ADP, these are hardly the tech stalwarts in the headlines. Even IBM and ADP don't come to mind when thinking about the high-growth tech leaders of today. We aren't interested in the hotshot tech businesses like those represented by FANG stocks. There are several reasons we don't invest in headline tech stocks, including their volatility, but mostly because they don't pay a dividend. We like to be paid to wait. We also have more conviction in company earnings when the business shares those earnings as dividends with the owners. In addition, multiyear growing dividends have special appeal because they show management's conviction in the persistence and sustainability of earnings. Finally, regular growing dividends tend to take the edge off a firm's price volatility. It's kind of a safety net for the business's market value. That's just the Make Your Family Rich mindset.

We realize that many tech companies have not been around that long and have only relatively recently started paying dividends. We created a list of tech companies that we believe are the meat and potatoes of the tech industry that have been paying increasing dividends from when they started making distributions. Furthermore, we believe that given enough time, these Dividend Champion Wannabes will make it to their twenty-fifth anniversary and keep going from there. The businesses in our Wannabe list below and the relevant data are drawn from Justin Law's Dividend Challenger list (ten to twenty-four years of increasing dividends). We love this guy. Send him a Valentine's Day greeting. It's OK, even if you're a guy.

Here are our Wannabes with the same data as before:

Trading Symbol	Name	# Years	Annual Rate
AAPL	Apple Inc.	11	9.2%
ADI	Analog Devices Inc.	20	11.0%
AVGO	Broadcom Inc.	12	43.6%
CSCO	Cisco Systems Inc.	11	23.4%
MCHP	Microchip Technology Inc.	21	2.1%
MSFT	Microsoft Corp.	20	13.0%
ORCL	Oracle Corp.	13	18.0%
TXN	Texas Instruments Inc.	18	22.4%
QCOM	QUALCOMM Inc.	20	12.5%

All are great companies. You see what we mean about the meat and potatoes. Does anyone seriously doubt that all these will meet the twenty-five-year Dividend Champion threshold? We tend to think of the products of these businesses like the jeans and mining equipment of the Gold Rush. Those were the guys selling the durable clothes and gold panning equipment needed by all those fellows trying to strike it rich in the fields. We don't know much about gold mining or panning, but we do know something about the business and investing moats that constantly increasing dividends create.

We own most of these businesses, and we've sold put options on all of them when they dipped a lot. As inflation and interest rates have headed north during the first part of 2022, the tech stocks have gone down more than the general market, so we've been picking up some of these businesses at what we consider nice prices.

The Random STI

I don't like to admit this, but there's the rare occasion when I have the itch to sell a put on a random business. If Citicorp (C) drops to a particularly low price relative to its book value, we may put in a bid on a put. OK, we did it again recently after the federal government used JP Morgan Chase (JPM) to restructure the failing regionals. How far wrong can you go selling JPM put strikes at $25 when the market price is $38, even if the price to book is about 1.4? Looks to us like JPM is the government's go-to big bank. Besides, where do you think all those deposits flying out of regionals are going? You see, that's the kind of thinking that can get you in trouble when you believe you're smarter than Mrs. Market, but that itch was really bugging me.

The same is the case with great pharmaceutical companies like Pfizer (PFE) or Bristol Meyers (BMY). The itch just gets to me sometimes, but only on a day when stocks like these drop a lot. If we actually get the stock, we don't DRIP it and start selling calls almost right away. Sometimes I wait for it to pop up a bit before I sell a call—usually about 15% higher than the current price. I never plan to hold the stock indefinitely. These random STIs don't qualify as the businesses we want to own forever, but when we see an opportunity, we try to capitalize on that. These STIs always eventually get sold, but often only after we've sold calls a couple of times. We milk them before they get sold off. I sometimes tell Matt and Erin we have a dairy side business.

Don't STI a Lot

So, scratch the itch when you must. It might drive you nuts if you don't scratch. Always employ the same acquisition techniques. That is, sell a put option if available on a down day. We find it wise to limit our STI put selling and stock acquisitions. The STIs just don't meet that Dividend Champion standard. We tend to make an exception for the Wannabes and acquire them almost at the same pace as the Dividend Champions. But the random STIs, not so much. You will likely have your own STIs. But if you do STI, then our advice is to limit your options sales and stock acquisitions. You might also want to employ our practice of selling calls once an STI is acquired. If your STI acquisition doesn't work, just consider it tuition in your MYFR refresher course.

7

HOW TO CONTROL
THE GNU IN YOU

R EMEMBER THAT PETER LYNCH QUOTE, "THE most important body part in investing is the stomach, not the brain." This chapter will help you understand how the MYFR system operates to control your stomach.

What's this about gnus? Those are the strange-looking African antelopes, also called wildebeests. I remember seeing a video of a huge herd of gnus somewhere out on the Serengeti. The gnu is a staple in a lion's diet, and once a pride of lions shows up, the word goes out, and the gnu herd stampedes. They all boogie in one direction until they end up in the Zambezi River, fall off a cliff to their death, or end up on the lion buffet. It never works out well for the gnus when the lions show up and start a stampede.

When you manage your investments in the conventional way—keeping score of your performance by the value of your portfolio—there's a strong incentive to act like a gnu. We call it the Gnu Effect. You've probably seen it many times. When the stock market declines by 10% or 20%, investors start to panic, and the temptation to sell can become overwhelming. That's not what the investment-wise men and women tell you to do.

We've all heard the old saying attributed to Baron Rothschild, the eighteenth-century British nobleman and member of the Rothschild banking family, "The time to buy is when there's blood in the streets." Easy to say. Find someone with the Peter Lynch-style stomach that actually does that. Once a market goes down, a lot of folks tend to act more like gnus, and that makes sense when you keep score by value.

The MYFR system helps you act more like a lion than a gnu. Let me recount some of the features of the MYFR system that encourages lionlike behavior in a steep-down market:

1. You are mostly limiting acquisitions to Dividend Champions. Remember, Dividend Champions are those higher-quality businesses that have paid increasing dividends for at least twenty-five years. The relatively dependable income generated by the Champions tends to limit their volatility. That is, the increasing dividend flow has the effect of calming the passions that drive investors to sell when markets drop. The tendency of a stock to perform relative to the market is measured as the stock's beta. A beta of 1.0 means the stock is likely to rise or fall in sync with the market. A beta lower than 1.0, say 0.7, means the stock can be expected to rise or fall at a rate of 70% of the market. A beta of 1.3 indicates a more volatile stock that rises or falls at a rate of 30% higher or lower than the market. The lower the beta, the less likely you act like a gnu.

2. With the MYFR system, you aren't directly buying the Dividend Champions but selling out-of-the-money put options. That's an important difference because you're being paid to buy into Baron Rothschild's bloody street. Even more important, as the market drops, out-of-the-money put option premiums seem to increase, so the incentive to sell puts logically increases.

Let me expand on that idea using the insurance analogy for put options. When you sell a put, you're committing to buy the underlying stock if it declines below the strike price on a future date. In a down market, the put buyer, or the other side of the transaction, is getting a guarantee that you, the put seller, will buy his stock at the reduced price if the stock continues to decline. That is, you (the put seller) are providing the put buyer an insurance policy to buy his interest if the value declines below the strike price.

Think of it as a guy with a nice cabin on top of a mountain in California. The cabin is fully paid for, so there's no mortgage company that requires property loss coverage. But you, the cabin owner, are increasingly concerned as forest fires become more prevalent in the area. The greater the incidence of fires, the higher the premium you're willing to pay for the insurance. That's the way puts work. The market is declining, so stock owners want to make sure they're covered against catastrophic loss, and you, the put seller on Dividend Champions, have your side out-of-the-money put-selling insurance gig. It might help to think of put-selling this way: When there's a fire sale in the stock market, insurance premiums (put option prices) go up.

3. In a down market, if you're selling puts, you're offering to buy the stock at a substantially lower price than the current price. Say the market is down 20%, and **XYZ** company is down 20% to $100. You likely will be selling a put with a strike price of around $85. It's easier to buy into the bloody street when your commitment is at an even lower price than the reduced market price that caused all that blood to flow.

4. This may be the most important point in avoiding the gnu effect. You, the MYFR system practitioner, keep score of your success by *income*, not *value*. So, when the market declines—and even when it declines a lot—you don't care. Ac-

tually, that's not true. You will always care when the market declines. But that concern will be mitigated by your confidence that your income will continue to increase regardless of market declines. Why? Because you own only Dividend Champions, and you have confidence in their consistently increasing dividends. And if you are DRIPping those dividends, you have turbocharged your constantly increasing dividend income. Look, we have been fortunate to be able to DRIP almost all our dividends. But sometimes, and particularly when taxes are due, we may need cash and might unDRIP some investments. In those cases, it's just as easy to unDRIP some investments as it was to originally DRIP them. Turning DRIPs on and off is simple.

5. You get a second bite at the apple. You, the out-of-the-money put seller, have many opportunities before the option expires to "sell to cancel," which is the expression used to describe the reversing of your option sale. That is, you can cancel your obligation to buy the stock at the strike price. If you "buy to cancel," you may sustain a loss depending mostly on whether the price of the underlying stock has risen or fallen since you sold the put. In any event, if a loss is incurred, it will usually be significantly less than if you had bought the shares of the stock.

The features of the MYFR system not only help the business owner avoid selling into a down market but also encourage the exact practice recommended by Baron Rothschild those many years ago.

Dividend Champions Are the Antidote to the Gnu Effect

Think about March of 2020, when the pandemic panic took hold of the media, the country, the world, and the markets. Markets dropped about 35%! Many folks, fearing even further decline, sold—and into the Zambezi they went. But the market actually recovered relatively quickly. Think about what you would have done if you were keeping score of your performance by your income. Using the Make Your Family Rich system, you would have had the confidence that no matter the precipitous drop, your income would increase.

You're still going to be anxious about large market drops. There can never be a 35% decline without anxiety. But because you have the discipline to measure performance by income, you'll know and take comfort from the fact that your income will increase. It's not how you feel that matters so much. It's what you do, and you're not a gnu! You can structure your asset management business so that your income increases no matter what. With that confidence, you're much less likely to sell and stampede with all those gnus to a terrible fatal fate.

Hang-in-There Approach

Where I live, there's a financial advisor who has a regular weekend radio show. The host is the owner and operator of a business that offers investment advisory services around the region. He says he saw rough times coming for the market early in 2022 and advised his clients to reduce their equity exposure. By summer 2022, that was a smart call because the market was down by about 20%. He criticizes other financial advisors who, in a down market, advise their clients to "hang in there."

During each show, he routinely condemns what he calls the hang-in-there approach. He apparently made the right sell recommendation, but that also requires he make the right purchase call to get his clients back in at the right time. In retrospect, he's proud of the sell call, but it only makes sense for his clients if he also makes the right purchase call. That's one of the great problems with keeping score of your success by the value of your portfolio. You must be a good market timer. You must know when to buy *and* when to sell. Can anyone really do that consistently?

The MYFR system actually embraces the hang-in-there approach. When you measure success by your constantly increasing income, why wouldn't you hang in there when your estimated annual income increases every month? That's one of the great advantages of the MYFR system. We buy our businesses forever or for so long as they continue to give us raises. We aren't constantly churning and trying to play the ups and downs of the market. We aren't timing the market. Our timespan is forever, and we have control of our gnu.

8

INVEST ONLY IN AMERICA, WELL, ALMOST

THERE ARE GOOD REASONS ALL THOSE PEOPLE want to move to the United States. We may have our problems, but who doesn't? Make no mistake: this is the land of unlimited opportunity. My parents knew that, and that's why they beat a path to the US. How about this guy Elon Musk—from South Africa to the richest guy in the world in one generation? Do you figure that would have happened if he had stayed in South Africa or Canada?

Forget all the Divisiveness

I heard one of those commentators at the border say that they've counted migrants from more than 150 countries coming across our southern border. Our homegrown liberal cynics can go on about the country's white supremacy and systemic racism, but those pictures of folks streaming into the country seem to include people of all different complexions.

I recently drove across the south from Florida to central Texas. I made lots of stops along the way. We own McDonald's stock (MCD has paid an increasing dividend for forty-six years), and I love the restaurants, particularly the free refills and the Wi-Fi. I bet I stopped at about every fifth MCD along the route.

I'm one of those guys who talks with everyone. If I'm in line at a McDonald's or the gas station convenience store, I'll find something to talk about with the guy in front of me and the one behind. It's just what I do. In the last couple of COVID years, people spent a lot of time at home watching television, reading, and working online, so I really like getting back out there.

The senior's price for MCD's coffee was running about seventy-nine cents. So, whenever I sprung for a $2 cup of coffee at a gas station, I always asked, "Does your family know you charge a senior citizen living on a fixed income $2 for a cup of coffee?" I love doing that, and the reactions I get range from an indulgent smile reaction to a serious, "I don't decide the prices, sir."

At a gas station in Louisiana, the sales lady was an older Black woman, and I received a neat smile to my wise-guy remark. "It's on the house, sweetie," she said. I got a kick out of that, and I also wondered if she understood that was a sexist remark. It was only for a nanosecond, but the thought did cross my mind. She and I chatted for a bit, and as I drove away, I kept thinking about my ridiculous nanosecond reaction. It seems modern American life and the media fixation on racial, sexual, and any other type of divisive identification has us all conditioned to characterize even the simplest human interactions with a judgmental, negative caste. The lady gave me a cup of coffee, and we enjoyed each other's company for a couple of minutes. Color, station in life, and education didn't matter—just two Americans in a gas station.

I really enjoyed my long three-day drive. Everyone was nice to me, and I couldn't help but reflect on how different my experience was from how so many have come to think of our country and how divided we supposedly are. No one will ever accuse me of being sensitive, but I did not see the division. But then, I also don't know any racists. I don't know a single white person who wouldn't hire a

Black person because they're Black. I don't know a white person who wouldn't befriend a Black person because he or she is Black. I'm sure there are racists out there—white folks who don't like Black people simply because they're Black. If that's true, then it is also likely that there are Black people who don't like whites because they are white. But that's not the rule; I think that's a rare exception. My suspicion is we will always have people like that, and there's not much you can do about that. Probably just better to ignore them. There's certainly not much the government can do about how people feel about their neighbors.

The 1969 World Series

I like to think of America as one big 1969 World Series event. I was there at the Polo Grounds and was working on opening day in 1961 with the new Mets. I was also there on opening day in 1964 at Shea Stadium in Queens. I left New York to move to Washington, DC, to take a job and start law school in the summer of 1965. The Mets were really bad news at this baseball thing. Their early manager, Casey Stengel, summed it up in his famous rhetorical question, "Can anyone here play this game?"

In 1969, never having had a winning season and never finishing better than ninth in their ten-team division, the Amazin' Mets went to the big show against the American League's Baltimore Orioles. I think my most enduring memory of that World Series is that everyone was a Mets fan. Even if you were from Baltimore, you were at least a closet Mets fan. That's just the way Americans are. Rooting for the underdog is what we do. Because, in a way, either we or our forebears were underdogs at some point. The Mets took the Series in five games! Ed "Kid" Kranepool, born and bred in the Bronx, was there with the Mets. Kranepool had been brought up by the Mets in 1962 at age seventeen, and he was a natural favorite among my Bronxite friends who worked in the ballparks and me.

There's a point in all this. We all know the history of Black folks in the United States. Today, I think pretty much everyone is rooting for them. But I don't think most folks want to see or deal with their Black fellow citizens as victims. We want to deal with Black folks like everyone else, and we want them to have the same opportunities that we all have as Americans. There's a reason lots of those people streaming over the border are people of color. It's because they know America is where it's at. Remember that expression the historically Black universities used to use in their fundraising: "A mind is a terrible thing to waste." I think that's the way we, as Americans, should think about all our people. It's not good for any of us or the country if any one of us or any group of us does not have the opportunity to fulfill our potential. But it's *opportunity*, not *preference*. I think most Americans believe no one should be given preference based on race or sex or anything else other than merit.

Many Black Americans live in our big cities. That's where I grew up, too—in the Bronx. I think many of our urban schools and city leaders should be ashamed of themselves. You've heard the numbers. Things like, "Only 10% of the sixth-grade students in City X perform at grade level." There's a whole bunch of minds being wasted there. If children aren't performing at their grade level, they should be kept after school to be tutored and tested until they get up to and beyond the grade level. Parents should be called into school in the evening and told their children are not cutting the academic mustard, and the parents should be held accountable for overseeing their children's homework—and students need to be given lots of homework. If public schools don't get the children to perform at grade level, then parents need to be able to send their children to alternative schools, including church-based schools. That's what my parents did. All their children went to Catholic schools in the Bronx. I like to think of those schools back then as the original charter schools.

I've never been more positive about America. I think all those people streaming across the border have it right. This is where you want to be regardless of sex, race, or religion. I'm deeply grateful to my parents for immigrating to America, and all their descendants have done well here.

There's one other thing that bugs me. It's the growing view that America has shortages of certain skills and that we should give preference in immigration to those with advanced degrees. I don't like that. If we need guys and gals with advanced degrees, then the country needs to grow them. An India-born guy with a degree in computer science from an Indian university might be readily employable in America, but he made his academic bones in India. It might be that his commitment to America is less than the person who gets here with nothing and then acquires the right education or guides his children to get that education and qualifications. That's how my parents and our family did it. I think everyone can do well in America, and pretty much everyone can become rich, particularly if they embrace the MYFR system.

Let's get back to that discrimination thing. If you really believe that being an African American or Hispanic or a female or whatever else is an impediment to getting rich, understand that applying the MYFR system has nothing to do with any of that. There's really no place or opportunity for discrimination. All the data necessary to implement the system is blind regarding who uses the information. Most of the implementation is done in cyberspace, and your computer doesn't know anything about your personal characteristics.

An MCD's Teaching Opportunity

I believe we all have an obligation to resist this scourge to convince our people, and particularly the next generation, that we are a racist society or that our people exploit poor folks. There are bad folks, and there will always be bad folks. But this is a great country of unlimited opportunity.

My favorite restaurant is McDonald's. I know it's not real food, and you should never eat fast food. I get all that, but I like the MCD's fare. I like the prices, and I even like the app—and I sure like the folks who work there. MCD has great Wi-Fi and free refills, and because most folks now go through the drive-through, there's plenty of space in their light and bright restaurants. That's where I meet my colleagues during the day to discuss business; we all call it "the office." We have a favorite spot—the long "conference table" with the high stools. Did I mention we own stock in MCD, which has paid an increasing dividend for forty-six years? Forty-six years!

I was seated at the conference table not too long ago, laptop out, talking investments with some of my senior homeboys. At a table nearby, I could see the restaurant manager interviewing a young fellow I figured to be about sixteen. After a while, she left him to fill out the forms and returned to the kitchen. Look, I never pass up an opportunity to do my lecture on how great this country is and how special McDonald's is.

So, this big old white guy sat down where the manager had been, and I said, "Do you know many years ago, the second richest guy in the world sat where you're sitting, doing exactly what you're doing—filling out a McDonald's job application? That bald guy was Jeff Bezos, who created Amazon. Bezos has more money than anyone in the world except only one other guy, and Bezos started right where you are in New Jersey when he was about sixteen."

To that, I got something that sounded like, "Huh."

Leave it at that? Not on your life! "Do you know that one in eight Americans will work at McDonald's during their life? Do you know what percentage that is? It's 12.5% of all Americans. It's the best place ever to start working."

Am I good or what? Maybe not so good as much as scary. Anyway, our young applicant caught his breath and finished filling out the forms, then brought them to the counter. End of the story? Not a chance.

A little while later, our now hopefully aspiring and ambitious capitalist approached the conference table. I could see he had something to say, so I went over to him. Quietly, he said, "I'm hungry."

Did I feel sorry for him? Not a chance. What a great opportunity to launch into phase two of my American capitalism spiel. Maybe this young fellow was a plant by the American Capitalism Society or one of those radical right-wing groups. I reached into my wallet and handed him a coupon for a Big Mac and another for a large fries. Then I asked provocatively, "Know where I got those?"

When our young fellow answered in the negative, I said, "My family owns part of the McDonald's business. We own stock in MCD. I don't like the way the ordering on the kiosk works, so I wrote a letter to the head guy in Chicago who runs all the McDonald's restaurants. I told him how to improve things, and he said he'd work on the kiosk thing and sent me these coupons. One day, you can own part of McDonald's. If you go to work for McDonald's here, I'll show you how to be an owner."

A couple of minutes later, he was back with the Big Mac but no French fries. He told me they would only take one coupon at a time, and he offered to return the fries coupon. I told him to keep it and use it next time.

I often wonder what happened to that young fellow. I hope that whatever bad deal he came into the office with that day, he left feeling that there were lots of opportunities out there for him, and maybe that big old white guy might just be like all Americans who were really on his side.

Concentrate on the Land of Opportunity

My first book, *Make Your Family Rich: Why to Replace Retirement Planning with Succession Planning*, details many of my personal experiences while traveling around the world. Color me an ugly American, but I can't get comfortable with investing anywhere else. I know all that stuff about global diversification, but I don't see the advantage.

Many of the Dividend Champions have significant sales around the world, and some have most of their sales in the international market. Some countries like China are believed to be growing their economies faster than the US, and investment advisors often recommend investing in China to tap into the advantages of that more rapid growth.

I don't buy that, as discussed in my earlier book. First, it's a government-controlled economy run by communists, and I don't believe any of their data or trust their leadership. I think of Chinese leadership as CINO—that's Capitalists In Name Only. Chairman Xi just got anointed to a third term as president. He's also head of the Chinese Communist Party. Years ago, Communist leadership embraced capitalist business practices supposedly to raise folks out of poverty, and it worked. Now there's a surprise. China has made enormous economic progress. But now that China has incredibly wealthy people like Jack Ma, the former schoolteacher and founder of Alibaba, the commies must make sure they all get back in line. You got it; that wasn't the accomplishment of all those businesspeople; that success was attributed to the commies.

I remember seeing Jack Ma on TV the day his company was listed on the New York Stock Exchange. That was one ebullient Chinaman! Jack seemed to be everywhere on the NYSE floor and was the most likable guy on the planet. I also remember thinking, How can his commie overlords allow this? Then his Michael Jackson extravaganza that was piped around the world had to be just too much for the commies. How could capitalism continue to be tolerated with that kind of excess? Michael Jackson already! This guy was way too gringoized and had to be kung pao chickened. There probably is some CCP fortune cookie aphorism that says, "Let no greedy money changer outshine the commie sun he orbits." Then Jack seemed to disappear. He probably went in for "retraining."

We've been to China a couple of times. I very much like the people, and they seem to understand and like the US. Many want to come to the US and send their children here to be educated. But if so many of their successful people want to come to the US, why would I want to send my money there? I think if you want to tap into the growth in China and sales in China or elsewhere in the world, then you should own MCD, JNJ, PG, and a host of other great American Dividend Champions with a strong presence in global markets.

Neither do I believe that the great innovations that will drive future growth will originate in other countries, and that's a good reason to invest in foreign markets. That's just not the way it seems to work. The folks with great ideas are either already in America or they are coming here with their great ideas. Think Elon Musk. Then look at the more competitive American US education institutions and see how many Asians are there. I attended the graduation of our grandson from one of the more academically competitive high schools in Austin, Texas, a couple of years ago, and more than half the top ten students were of Asian descent. Do you figure those youngsters are hightailing it back to Asia anytime soon with all their great ideas? That is not the way I see it. My bet is that those students and their creative skills are staying right here. So, if you can tap sales in growing foreign markets and the best innovation by investing in great American companies, why push to invest globally?

Then there's just plain old simplicity. There are about 7,000 US public companies, which make up about 12% of the public companies worldwide. You can't keep track of that many businesses. The MYFR system focuses on just the 143 Dividend Champions. That's a diverse lot across multiple industries with plenty of business around the world. One hundred forty-three of the right businesses is plenty, particularly when they're all focused on increasing the income they distribute to you every year. Do you still want foreign? Buy a nice Italian chianti and get over investing in foreign companies. Okay, a couple of the Dividend Champions are foreign based. There's Canadian National Rail (CNI). Guess where they call home. Need something more exotic? How about Medtronic (MDT) based in Ireland? MDT is really a gringo company but headquartered in Ireland as a tax dodge. We own both.

Forget All the Social Engineering Stuff

For some time now, there have been investment advisors promoting various ideas for investing to promote one social agenda or another. The most common seems to be the various causes expressed in the acronym ESG. That stands for environmental, social, and corporate governance. Those advisors promoting ESG want you to believe that they'll help you invest to achieve their environmentally signif-icant results and to advance various social justice causes. Do you really believe that some ESG financial analyst can do a better job of determining how best to comply with the legal and regulatory norms of our country than the leadership of our great American businesses? In terms of governance, they promote causes like more racially diverse and sexually inclusive corporate governance. They would like you to believe that pursuing ESG objectives is good for business in the long run.

The purpose of your asset management business is to own an array of businesses that generate constantly increasing dividends for their owners. To do that, the businesses must generate profits that confidently increase over time. You do not want to own businesses where the managers have a different goal than generating constantly increasing profits. If you owned a professional sports team, your ob-jective would be to win games. You don't want a manager who loses games only to tell you that winning doesn't matter as long as you have the right racial mix on your team.

Remember that the MYFR system involves owning great Amer-ican businesses. Those are businesses almost entirely headquartered in the US and, therefore, are subject to US regulation and over-sight. The US government and the states are aggressive regulators of businesses within their borders. The US Environmental Protec-tion Agency (EPA) provides the environmental regulatory structure under which businesses must operate within the country. The US Department of Labor and the Equal Employment Opportunity Commission and their local counterparts provide for the regulation and enforcement of labor standards. Similarly, the US Securities and Exchange Commission monitors the integrity of corporate leadership in managing their businesses in ways that comply with the full range of the various regulatory regimes. What more do you want? Do you really believe some financial analyst can do a better job of determining who best complies with legal and regulatory norms than the public agencies responsible for regulating businesses?

Look, if you have a personal objective not to invest in a certain business or industry, then do that. For example, Altria (MO) is a tobacco company Dividend Champion, and if you have an aversion to all things about smoking, you might not want to own MO. Similarly, if you dislike some business or political bias an individual Dividend Champion has, then don't invest with them.

I have the same view with respect to corporate management that promotes DEI in their corporate cultures. DEI stands for diversity, equity, and inclusion. It's mostly about creating corporate staff that will ensure that the business inculcates DEI into its leadership's decision-making. My view is that corporate cultures should be meritocracies. That is, people should be selected, developed, and advanced based on their merit and contributions to the success of the business. Why waste valuable capital on the development of staff that doesn't directly contribute to the profitability of the corporate enterprise? My way of thinking is that DEI staff increase overhead, which reduces the profitability of the business.

I have strong reservations about our country and our investment strategies when decisions are based on who you are in terms of sex or race. Historically, we've been a country, society, and economy that rewards what you can accomplish. New ethnic groups coming to our shores typically started at the lowest rungs in our ladder of success. They had to prove themselves to move up that ladder. That has always made sense to me, and that proof was accomplished by advancing one's skills through education and hard work. Ours is a selfish economy. Success is achieved by creating value for an employer or business owner. You achieve advancement by creating success and profit for others, not because of your gender or race.

The Zero Denominator Guy

Only in America does it pay to be born as a Zero Denominator Guy (ZDG). A ZDG is a person who is born poor. In most places in the world, you die where you are born, economically speaking. In the US, you have the best chance to grow wealth, and if you die with a numerator, you've achieved an infinite rate of return. You got it: any number divided by zero is infinite.

A purpose of the MYFR system is to make your numerator high, very high. Being born a Zero Denominator Guy is a big advantage. Have you ever heard a guy running for office standing at a podium say, "I was born to a very rich family. I literally came into this world with a silver spoon in my mouth"? Of course not. Being born rich is a handicap in the political arena. It's like starting out on the road to life in the highest gear. Better to be born broke and aspire to everything. Then there's everything to achieve, and as you tick off those achievements, you'll feel great about yourself and the family you raise.

In this country, there are endless education opportunities. Get as much of that stuff as you can. In fact, nowadays, there's no reason to ever stop your education. All of that education is online, and you can access it almost any time. Forget watching television and playing video games. There's all that free and low-cost education out there. The more education a Zero Denominator Guy gets, the higher his or her numerator is likely to rise, particularly if they're following the MYFR system.

Here's another factor about America you don't hear much about. America is a great place to start a business—the best. But startups can have a high failure rate. Maybe you've heard the numbers. Something like half the new restaurants go under in the first couple of years. That's no reason not to start a business if you have the ambition. But pretty much everything has been securitized during my lifetime. You can buy an interest in someone else's business as an investor. By investing only in Dividend Champions, you can acquire a broad stable of successful businesses run by accomplished people. How do you know those folks are all that accomplished? Because they have paid increasing dividends to owners like you for at least twenty-five years, that's how!

9

DRIPPING: COMPOUND INTEREST TURBOCHARGED

THIS IS ONE OF THE BOOK'S SHORTEST CHAPTERS, but it's really important in your long-term planning to make your family rich. DRIP stands for Dividend Reinvestment Plan, and it's the fourth of the nine principles of the MYFR system. Not all public companies offer the DRIP option, but almost all Dividend Champions have the plans. A DRIP is simply the opportunity to take your dividends as proportionate shares of additional stock. Most Dividend Champions pay dividends quarterly, and if you choose to DRIP a particular business, then on the dividend payment date, your account is credited with more shares of the company. No muss, no fuss. You automatically increase the amount of the great businesses you own.

Let's say your quarterly dividend payment on a particular firm is $75, and the stock trades at $30 per share at the time of the dividend distribution. If you have chosen to DRIP your dividends, then you'll acquire an additional 2.5 shares of the business. Notice that when DRIPping, you can acquire fractional shares of the company.

I love DRIPs. They come as nice surprises during the business day. You check your account midday, and there you have this neat little gift. Even when you remember a dividend is due, it still comes as a bit of a surprise. Hardly a week goes by that we don't acquire additional DRIPped shares. Even if you aren't actively selling puts—and maybe the market is climbing and what puts you have out aren't striking—you're constantly acquiring a greater interest in the Dividend Champions you already own.

Think about the effects of compounding when you are DRIPping. Dividend Champions are always increasing their distributions to you, the owner of the company. That's what Dividend Champions do. Then add in the fact that you're constantly adding to your ownership, and you see why we say that DRIPping is compound interest turbocharged. Over time and with increasing dividends, you're buying an increasing interest in your businesses.

Perish the thought if you ever want to sell a Dividend Champion! But it could happen in the rare instance when a particular Dividend Champion fails to increase the dividend. In that case, we recommend a special way of disposing of the former Dividend Champion, as discussed in Chapter 10, "When and How to Sell." If we have only a fractional share left at the end of the day, Ameritrade buys the fractional shares based on the closing price for the stock on that day.

Unless you need income, DRIPping is the way to go. Typically there are no trading or transaction fees, and some companies offer a discount off the market price when exchanging the cash due to you for the DRIPped shares. If you can afford it, fight the urge to take the cash dividends. DRIPping is too powerful a tool not to use.

With our brokerage firm, TD Ameritrade, we have a simple way of choosing to DRIP a particular business. We can select firms to DRIP and collect cash dividends on others. It is a simple click to DRIP or unDRIP as your circumstances change over time.

There's one important consideration with respect to income taxes. Of course, dividend income is taxable. If, instead of cash, you receive additional stock, then the income equivalent is still taxable. Depending on your individual circumstance, you may need to take some or all of your dividend income in cash to pay the taxes due. Wouldn't it be great if the tax laws were revised so that DRIPped dividends were exempted from income tax? What a great way for the government to promote additional investment by Americans. Don't hold your breath so long as a liberal administration is in charge.

One final note. We are always DRIPping. With the market downturn in 2022, we generally have not been selling as many puts. That's a function of the reduced cash we have available. I don't like going on margin at a time of such uncertainty. I prefer to reserve our buying and leverage to a time when I see our economy in a more expansionary, optimistic phase. All that said, we continue to DRIP all our Dividend Champions. So, at a time when we're making limited new acquisitions, we still add to our ownership by using all our dividends to buy more shares. Why is that? Because, over time, we're always optimistic about the American business cycle and the long-term direction of our markets.

10

WHEN AND HOW TO SELL

T HE ANSWER TO THE QUESTION ABOUT WHEN to sell is easy. Never. Well, almost never. It's good to recap a couple of our principles. For example, we keep score of our success by our constantly increasing income. We achieve that kind of income by mostly investing in Dividend Champions. So if the businesses we own keep increasing our income, why would we ever sell? The increasing income and the way we measure success removes much of the incentive to do the gnu stampede when the market tanks.

All those stock pickers who measure success by the value of their portfolio are busy trying to pick winners. The guy who tries to pick those winners to buy must also be able to determine the losers so he or she knows when to sell. Getting a headache yet? That's not only a lot of work trying to be smarter than Mrs. Market, but who really believes they can determine not only when to buy but also when to sell?

The MYFR system dictates that we only sell when a Dividend Champion stops increasing its annual dividend. Simple rule. As long as the business keeps increasing our income, we keep DRIPping and accumulating more of the company. Rarely does a Dividend Champion stop paying an increasing dividend. When it does, we sell right away. Well, not quite. Let me try and explain that, and it involves selling options rather than the stock. Now don't panic on me. We got through all that selling puts on dips, right? You really liked that idea too, didn't you? Well, you're going to like selling covered call options too.

During the start of the pandemic panic back in the spring of 2020, the market collapsed by about 35%. Imagine how the gnus reacted when they saw that 35% lion headed their way. The value of your investments goes down more than a third in a matter of days and weeks! Can't you see those gnus stampeding toward that raging river? I was concerned, too. We did not go down 35%, but we went down a lot. You can't help but be concerned. But what's important is not how you feel but what you do. During that time, we did not sell; we did not stampede. In fact, we continued to sell out-of-the-money puts and eventually bought more businesses at even lower prices.

During the Rocket Recession starting in the spring of 2020, only two firms failed to increase their dividends. They were Ross Stores (ROST) and Helmerich and Payne (HP), the contract driller. Two out of the total of about 140! Did we sell them? Sort of. What we actually did was sell out-of-the-money, covered calls.

When a company interrupts its dividend increases, it can go down a lot. But even a business that has paid increasing dividends can have a bad spell. Retail operations and energy companies were particularly hard hit by the pandemic. Consumers significantly curtailed their in-store shopping, adversely affecting a retail operation like ROST. People also vastly reduced their driving, which resulted in reduced consumption of fuel. Very bad for both ROST and HP. That said, other retailers like TGT and WMT continued to increase dividends, as did energy companies like XOM and CVX. Why overthink it? ROST and HP stopped increasing their dividends.

What's a Call and How Does It Work?

Selling out-of-the-money covered calls is like being in the dairy business. "Out-of-the-money" means that in the case of calls, the strike price is above the current market price. "Covered" means you own the stock on which you are selling calls. You can sell "naked" calls meaning you don't own the stock, but that's a whole lot of risk you don't want.

Back to the dairy business metaphor. You own the cow, but rather than selling it for meat, you milk it for as long as you can before selling old Bossie. Let's say your Dividend Champion has stopped increasing its dividend. Before the announcement, the stock might have been priced at $80 and then dropped to $65 once there was a failure to increase the dividend. Calls, like puts, are sold in lots of 100 shares. Rather than sell the stock outright, a call lets you set a price higher (out-of-the-money) than the current price. For example, a three month call on a stock currently priced at $65 with a strike price of $72.50 three months hence might price for $2 per share for a total premium of $200. That's what we did with ROST and HP. We kept selling calls about 10% to 15% higher. When the calls expired unexecuted, we just resold them another two or three months forward. That's milking the cow until, on a future expiration date, the stock closes above the strike price, and the stock is called away from you. There's a bit of sadness in selling calls, knowing that one day a business that you once owned and had served you well will be gone.

Some folks routinely sell covered calls on businesses they own, even when they want to continue to own the company. It's an example of the old "everything is for sale at a price" principle. By setting a strike price 10% or 15% higher than the current market price, the owner is saying, "I don't think the price will increase that much that quickly, but if it does, I'm okay selling."

Some who focus on income see covered call premiums as a solid way to add to the regular cash flow they receive from their investments. We do sell covered calls on our Scratch the Itch (STI) investments. Remember, the STIs for us are often opportunistic purchases where we think a business is very underpriced. It's not a business we want to own forever like the Dividend Champions, but we may see an opportunity to make a quick return. Check out Chapter 6, "Scratch the Itch, But Not a Lot," for a fuller explanation.

If you look at the other side of the call contract, the fellow buying the call figures there will be a recovery in price, and for only $200, he can possibly acquire stock that could be worth a lot more than $72.50 on the expiration date. For example, if the stock on expiration date is selling at $80, he's made $550 on an investment of only $200. You compute that by comparing the market value on the expiration day of $8,000 ($80 x 100 shares) less the acquisition cost of $7,250 ($72.50 x 100). That's a $750 gross return on a $200 investment in two or three months. It's a net of $550 when you subtract the $200 paid from the $750 gain.

We never buy calls. Many investors believe that very few investors make a return buying calls, just like relatively few make money buying puts. We believe selling covered calls is a great way to dispose of a position when, in our rare case, it's time to sell a former Dividend Champion.

The characteristics of call selling are similar to put selling. The larger the business and the more active its stock trading, generally the more active the options trading. The more active the trading, the tighter the spread between the bid and ask prices.

Tax Advantage of Forever Investing

There's one more advantage to forever investing: you will save on the taxes that would be due when you sell with a gain. Substantial capital gains taxes on the profit could be due on sale. If you're a forever investor, you never pay capital gains taxes. In fact, at your passing, your heirs take your investments at the value upon your death. Capital gains can be a big bite and avoiding capital gains taxes gives you a long-term advantage in achieving the FINER life.

11

DEBT CAN BE YOUR FRIEND OR YOUR WORST ENEMY

I COULD EASILY BE A RESIDENT OF NOWHERESVILLE right now if not for access to debt. I started out with a job but no capital, so the availability of debt for my early investing was important. But make no mistake; I believe you should only use debt to invest in businesses or education, not buy stuff. I've never used debt to buy stuff. Never financed a car. I use credit cards a lot, but even when I started out broke, I never ran an unpaid balance. I always paid the balance every month. If I didn't have the money, I didn't buy the stuff.

And why wouldn't I use a credit card to buy stuff I had the money to pay for? Credit cards help keep a record of expenses, which is particularly helpful come tax preparation time. Did I mention those frequent flyer miles? The truth is, I love credit cards. I have one that gets me into one of those airline clubs. Look, the first chance you get to buy one of those airline club cards when you start to travel frequently, you should do it. It's an expense, but I love the free food and drinks, the comfy chairs, and the great internet connection. Being such a cheapskate, I waited too late in life to get a club card. Big mistake. I'm not one for self-indulgence but do indulge yourself in this one.

Real Estate Borrowing

I bought my first house at age twenty-one. I had two mortgages and a job. To fund the renovations, I placed another mortgage with my employer's credit union. It was tough, particularly when I started law school at night. But it all got done, and we made some money—not a lot, but enough to buy the second house. It had two mortgages, too, but it was in move-in condition.

That started me on a life of buying and selling rental property. I always leveraged my purchases with mortgages, and over time, my rental income helped pay off the mortgages. With the gradual appreciation of real estate, my net worth constantly increased.

I very rarely had a down year. I knew that because I always kept a personal financial statement (PFS), so I always knew my net worth over time. A sample PFS is provided in Appendix B. I needed a PFS not only for my personal interest but also to keep my lenders informed of my financial condition. But owning and managing real estate was lots of work, and I came to think of real estate as running a business rather than investing.

When you're as active in real estate investing as I was, it also becomes common to invest in mortgages, which is simply the debt version of real estate investing. I occasionally sold property and took back a mortgage from the buyer. Later, I became a so-called hard money lender, and I made loans to owners who had difficulty getting standard bank-financed mortgages. In real estate, just like in public securities markets, there were opportunities to own both equities like rental properties and debt instruments like mortgages. In both cases, whether directly investing in real estate equities or debt, it's a lot of work that requires plenty of time and skills.

During my lifetime of investing, real estate has radically changed. Most significantly, virtually every investment opportunity became securitized. That is, we can now invest in almost any form of real estate by owning a public security, usually in the form of a real estate investment trust (REIT). On the equity side, you can invest in businesses that own a wide range of real estate assets, from office buildings to shopping malls and medical buildings. How about data centers or billboards? There are REITs for them too. Farmland, hotels, quick service restaurants? There are REITs for all of them. There are also MREITs or REITS that invest in mortgages.

At the risk of being repetitious, I believe that if you like real estate, then the best way to invest is to *buy securities*. Just like the best way to invest in manufacturing or pharmaceuticals, or restaurants is to buy Dividend Champion securities in those industries.

With real estate, debt is relatively inexpensive and safe. Your real estate is the primary security for the mortgage loan. Usually, if you default on the loan, the value of the real estate is the lender's first recourse for recovery through a variety of techniques like foreclosure. But if the value of the real estate is inadequate to cover the debt, the debtor, which is usually the owner, is responsible for the balance to the full extent of the borrower's net worth. Ouch! Consequently, the more an owner borrows against the real estate, the more likely there may be a problem if the investment does not pan out.

I say real estate debt is safe because financial institutions generally put limitations on the percentage of debt they'll extend to a particular property. That is, most lenders limit leverage to 70% to 80%. That's called the loan-to-value ratio or LTV. Usually, that kind of LTV can be supported by the cash flow from the rent. Lenders will also typically make sure that both the property, if it's an investment property, and the borrower have the capacity to repay the loan.

Securities Borrowing is Different

Real estate values tend to go up relatively slowly, and they come down gradually, too. Because individual real estate properties are illiquid, they don't give the owner a strong sense of volatility. The owner may sense that his or her real estate properties are going up or declining in value, but they rarely feel that the change in value is precipitous. That's in strong contrast to securities markets where individual stocks are liquid, and market volatility can be very high.

You frequently hear it said among regular stock traders that "the market goes up on an escalator and down on an elevator." Just think about the advent of the COVID pandemic when in March 2020, the market dropped 35%. That's not an investor thinking his assets might have declined 35%. He was literally looking at statements that told him the value of what he owned was worth 35% less at the end of the month than it was at the beginning. That's volatility, and that's pain.

Well, it's pain if you think like most market investors. We MYFR business owners keep score and measure our success by income, and our estimated annual income went up in March 2020. Okay, it was still somewhat painful. But the pain doesn't matter as much as what you do. If the sharp drop in value makes you fearful that the next month will also be bad or worse, you might panic into selling. Remember the Gnu Effect? As discussed in Chapter 7, "How to Control the Gnu in You," is when an investor joins the stampede to exit the market to avoid even greater losses. If you measure success by income and income is going up, you're a whole lot less likely to join in the gnu stampede to sell.

Getting back to our discussion of debt and leverage, let's use some round numbers. Say an investor owns a securities account with $1,000,000 of total securities. Then imagine he's borrowed $400,000 against that account. That means the net equity value of his holdings is $600,000. If those were the numbers for a real estate investment or a couple of properties, that's a relatively safe capital structure. The owner would have a 40% LTV, and that's no problem in my experience.

But then, real estate values typically don't ride elevators down. In the case of a securities account, a 35% decline would bring the total portfolio down to $650,000, and because it's subject to $400,000 in debt, the net equity value is only $250,000 ($650,000 - $400,000).

That means the account owner has suffered a 50% decline in value in a single month. For most people, keeping score by value, that's Panicsville, as well it should be.

Margin Accounts Are Dangerous

The debt backed by securities is referred to as the *margin*. Most brokerage firms require their clients to apply for and qualify for a margin account. Typically, the margin balance is limited to 50% of the total account value. Don't even think about borrowing that much on margin. If there's a drop in market valuation and your margin balance goes above 50%, you must either infuse new money or sell securities. If you don't do either to cover your margin, you'll get what's called a margin call, and your broker will be authorized to sell stock in your account to bring your margin balance back within your authorized limit. He or she gets to decide which of your holdings they sell. You never want that to happen.

Increasing your margin balance can be tempting, particularly in an up market. The more leverage you have, the greater your rate of return in an appreciating market. If you don't have cash to put into your account, the temptation to use margin can be very dangerous. In the beginning, it's probably best to avoid the use of margin entirely.

We Use Margin But Very Sparingly

We have access to funds other than our securities accounts. As discussed, we still own some real estate. But real estate is relatively illiquid and cannot be sold or refinanced quickly to pay down the margin. But we are diversified regarding assets, and there's some comfort that we have some limited access to capital from alternative sources.

The management of our family's main securities account is now in the hands of the next generation, my children. The debt Matt and Erin incur tends to be the "potential" debt kind. I say potential because they use our margin availability as the backing to sell out-of-the-money put options on Dividend Champions. Let me try and give you an idea of what that means. Say a particular Dividend Champion is priced at $100, and on a particular day—maybe in a generally down market—it drops to $95. Matt and Erin may seize the opportunity to sell a put with a strike price of $82.50 three months into the future. Of course, a put contract consists of 100 shares, and let's say the premium they earn is $200. If that put is sold with cash available, that would mean the put seller would need to have $8,250 available to buy the stock in the event the option expires below $82.50 on the expiration date. In that case, you would compute the cash-on-cash return like this: $200/$8,250 = 2.42%.

Because the return is for three months (or a quarter of a year), multiplying the 2.42% yields an annualized return of 9.68%. Not a bad annual return in today's interest rate market.

Now let's see what happens if we use a margin account to back that same put sale. In that case, it's important to remember that no margin debt is incurred if the underlying stock is never bought. So, if the put expires above the strike price, you won't be required to buy the stock, and you get to earn the premium that was paid into your account the moment you sell the put. Let's look at the earlier computation assuming the same out-of-the-money put sale is backed by margin: $200/$0 = An Infinite Rate of Return.

It doesn't get any better than an infinite rate of return. Therein lies the temptation and the extreme danger. Why not just sell puts up to the maximum extent of available margin? Remember March 2020, when values collapsed by about 35%? In that case, you either must buy back the puts, which is called "buying to cancel," usually at a loss, or buy the stock and incur the margin debt. You do not want to be in that position.

All of that said about the dangers of using margin to buy stocks, we do sell puts up to a certain extent that are backed by our margin account. Matt and Erin maintain a worksheet that shows them the potential liability, and under normal circumstances, they won't sell puts that could eventually result in a margin balance of more than 20% of the value of our owned account.

Our asset management business consists of all those great Dividend Champions we own, and in selling puts as the means to add to our asset management business, we won't incur potential debt beyond 20%. That is, in the kind of language used in real estate investing, we won't exceed a potential LTV of 20%.

Debt has been my friend. I used debt more extensively when I started investing, but that entirely involved real estate. I'm much more comfortable with higher LTVs when the security is a relatively stable real estate asset. I'm a whole lot less comfortable with high LTVs when public securities are involved. Stock markets can be much more volatile over the short term, and I never want to risk a margin call and giving up control of my investment decision-making. In my investment journey, I've encountered several people who got anxious and were careless with debt. Many went bankrupt, and others were forced to sell their assets at a bad time, often losing years of accumulated gains. Significant securities market-secured debt is not the path we recommend to make your family rich.

12

IT TAKES A VILLAGE: THE MYFR VALUES

I F MY EARLY CRIMINAL RETAIL EXPERIENCE DID not disqualify me from that Supreme Court nomination, this chapter should do the trick. You're going to be reading some serious politically incorrect stuff. I kind of think of it as the tough love version of Hillary Clinton's book *It Takes a Village*. This is the stuff you used to hear from fathers and grandfathers.

One of the MYFR values is that you shouldn't transfer the valuables of your generation to the next generation until *the values* are successfully transferred. Of course, that means the successor generation should accept the philosophy of the MYFR system of creating and maintaining wealth. But it also means the next generation should embrace the values by which we live. The two, the investment philosophy and lifestyle values, are related, if only indirectly.

College is for Everyone

I was on a local zoning board for several years. The guys used to get together afterward for dinner. I remember when one of the wiser and older fellows talked about his fourteen-year-old grandson and said he was "not college material." I about choked on my fried pickle. I've heard that a lot in recent times. I remember responding, "Bobby, how in the world do you know that? At fourteen, who knows what capabilities a youngster has or will have? If you're telling him that now, you can be assured that's how he'll think about himself, and when his time comes, he won't think of himself as college material."

All the data indicates that education directly correlates to life-time earnings. High school graduates make more than non-graduates. Folks with some college or college graduates make more than high school graduates, and folks with graduate degrees make more still. Then those with professional degrees make even more. Simple as that. Duckduckgo it.

Education correlates to everything positive—lower substance dependence, lower crime rates, and an educated person probably makes for a better citizen and parent. As a parent and grandparent, the MYFR value is to encourage all your successors to get as much education as they possibly can, and it's your job to make sure whatever capital is needed is available.

Even if the youngster eventually decides not to pursue more education, he or she should have an education ethic for their children. The best way to ensure that is to constantly emphasize the value of education. Maybe George Washington Carver said it best: "Education is the key to unlock the golden door of freedom."

Tattoos are Personal Graffiti

You want to emphasize to your heirs and successors that personal accomplishment is important and is the right way to achieve recognition. Everyone wants to be recognized in their community. Positive ways for a youngster to achieve recognition are educational accomplishment, success in sports, participation in community and church, volunteer activities, having a productive job, and just being friendly and helpful among neighbors. Those are all ways to achieve positive recognition.

Then there are lots of ways to achieve negative recognition. Just today, at the grocery store, I saw a young fellow about eight years old who had a purple Mohawk haircut. That's a child and presumably a parent who says, "Look at me." Look at me because I'm different, not because of my achievements, but because I'm the only person dumb enough to have a purple Mohawk.

This crazy, negative "look at me" syndrome is particularly rampant among the growing tattooed masses. I call tattoos personal graffiti. I often ask young people, no matter how creative a tattoo "artist" is, if that guy owned a house would he be dumb enough to graffiti his own home? Why not? Simply because graffiti destroys the property's value. It has the same effect on people.

Have you ever seen one of those crazy prison shows? Everyone in prison has tattoos. Did they go to prison because of their tattoos? Of course not. But birds of a feather flock together, and they are in prison. Not all people with tattoos end up in prison, but it seems that all people in prison have tattoos. There's no causation between tattoos and crime and prison. But there is a correlation. Just like an overwhelming majority of the people in prison don't have college degrees. The lack of a college degree is not why they're in prison, but there's a definite correlation between education and prison. You don't want to do anything that correlates with prison.

In the past, I've also built a couple of restaurants, and I've worked in them too. There are lots of folks in that business with tattoos, and I never fail to tell them what I think. It's part of my "it takes a village" responsibility. It might be too late for them, but not for their children. To date, I have never had one pushback. I think they know that getting tattooed was a mistake. Sure, it could be they are just being nice to this old guy with a big mouth. But somehow, I think they may agree.

I gave my personal graffiti lecture to a young trainee at a FedEx office some time ago. The guy was then in his late twenties, and he had two daughters. He told me he'd had problems getting jobs because of the tattoos. During our conversation, he had on a long-sleeved shirt, but I could see his tattoos peeking out.

When I asked what he would tell his two daughters, he said, "First of all, we don't call them tattoos. We call them job killers."

Now there's a guy who learned the lesson. By the way, studies indicate that our guy is correct. Human resources managers indicate that tattoos and piercings reduce employment opportunities.

Then there was the young woman who thought her personal graffiti was different. That was because she got tattoos to memorialize significant events in her life. So, when her mom remarried, she celebrated her new stepdad's and her mom's newfound happiness with a tattoo. When she had her own children, she got tattoos with their names and birth dates. I tried to convince her that it might be a better idea to just keep a family album or maybe a diary, but no go with this lady. She wanted to be a walking memorial to all of what she believed were her family's significant events.

I remember back in the neighborhood all those years ago that Jewish parents had the answer. According to my friends, their parents told them that if they ever got a tattoo, they couldn't be buried in a Jewish cemetery. Back then, I could understand why that worked. Today, I probably should be outraged. Being non-Jewish, what's so terrible about being planted next to me? Look, if it works, I'll defer my outrage, but only on the tattoo issue.

One day you'll be interviewing with a guy like me for a job or a car loan. All the background on your personal graffiti isn't going to impress me. I'll simply think you have a habit of making bad judgments. Sorry about that. I know that's stereotyping. After all, there are the likes of Angelina Jolie, and she's loaded and tatted up, too. Maybe you could be the next Ms. Jolie. See you in the movies.

Language as Verbal Personal Graffiti

If you use foul language, it says as much about you as your tattoos. It brands you as a guy or gal who has bad judgment. There's nothing that can be said with foul language that can't be said with standard language. All those tattooed guys in the prison yard have almost no ability to talk in conventional language. That's not why they're in prison, but most of those guys have repulsive vocabularies. Again, the guy interviewing for a loan or a job or for school admission is probably more like me, and that kind of language is a turnoff.

You'll be the owner of a growing asset management business, and you should look and sound like one. Check out the folks on CNBC and Bloomberg and listen to the way they speak. You want to talk like them. People who own businesses use the vocabulary of business. You should, too.

You Are What You Read and Watch

The more time you spend in a library, the better and more prosperous person you will be. I have zero data to prove this, but I've spent a lifetime around libraries, and I know that all the good stuff is there. Good people, too, from what I can tell.

To be successful at the MYFR system, it will help to know and speak the language of business. You find that in publications like the *Wall Street Journal* and *Barron's*. Most libraries have those publications, and you should be reading them. If they don't have the print edition, you should ask the librarian if they have the digital version. If they have neither, then you should ask them to get subscriptions—at least to the digital version.

At home, you should have CNBC Business or Bloomberg on during the day. They cover trading on the markets and are constantly interviewing various business leaders and analysts. Some of those business leaders will be the people who run the companies you own. Those guys work for you! If you're just starting out investing, it may all come across as so much Greek. But isn't that the way everything new starts? Remember, the purpose here is to make your family rich, and that will take some effort.

While you're at the library, ask them where they keep *Value Line*. That's a great publication that's usually kept in three-ring binders and is updated periodically with new inserts. I've been reading *Value Line* for more than forty years. It's a great service, and many libraries have *Value Line* in digital form. *Value Line* is not how we select our investments, but we do periodically check their analysis of various Dividend Champions and Wannabe Dividend Champions. Their analyses and ratings may also influence how many options we sell. Most libraries keep *Value Line* in a reference section, and they often require identification if you want to take a copy to your seat. For me, that's my driver's license. If you notice, the users of *Value Line* are mostly old guys like me. If you're a young investor, my bet is you'll become the buzz among the librarians if you check out *Value Line*. Imagine the confusion if you're a teen who wants to check out *Value Line* and don't have a driver's license. Talk about recognition!

Open a Brokerage Account

If you don't have a brokerage account, you need to open one pronto. You are a do-it-yourself guy, so you don't need financial advisory services. There is no need to pay those fees. You'll want to know what the firm's transaction fees are. Most firms now open commission-free stock trading, and you want to confirm that. You'll also be trading options, mostly selling puts, and you should confirm what that fee is. We pay sixty-five cents for an options sale. It's not that much, but make sure you know your fee. The big difference is usually in margin rates. The rate will typically vary depending on your margin balance. The higher the balance, the lower the rate. Margin rates are also variable. As short-term rates rise or fall, so will your margin rate.

Everything about your brokerage account is negotiable. If you don't ask and push, you'll pay the retail rack rates. As you might expect, when your account is relatively small, you have less negotiating leverage. As your account grows and your transactions increase, your negotiating juice increases. Your negotiating position also increases as a function of how many other folks you steer to your brokerage firm. However, your rates and fees will pretty much remain what they were on day one when you opened that small account unless you request lower rates. When requesting those lower rates, you'll need to show that better rates are available at other competitive firms. It's okay to put some romance into those competitive numbers, if you know what I mean.

By the way, the best rates seem to be available from Interactive Brokers (IBKR). That's the firm founded by Thomas Peterffy. He's that Hungarian immigrant billionaire who's the antidote to that crazy socialist Hungarian George Soros. Love this guy, Peterffy, and if I was starting out today, I'm sure I'd be with IBKR. Peterffy is the world's greatest anti-socialist, pro-capitalism guy. But I've been with TD Ameritrade and its predecessor since forever. And yet, I've used Thomas's IBKR margin rates to negotiate down my TDA rates. Thanks, Tommy. Check out Peterffy's *Wikipedia* bio. If you ever get shaky about the incredible opportunities America offers, everyone should read this guy's background. Think of Peterffy as the securities version of Elon Musk.

Your Politics

I tend to favor market solutions to societal problems. I tend to also think that American industry sees opportunity in the country's problems. When a rare or new disease presents itself, our pharmaceutical industry will invest in research funding and smart people to create a solution. Our tech firms constantly develop new devices and software to meet evolving problems. Today, innovation in space research and travel is mostly led by private firms. Personal transportation innovation seems to be led by the likes of Elon Musk and his Tesla firm. Sure, the government subsidizes the purchase of electric vehicles, but the innovation comes from industry. I believe that even electricity generation, if left to the private sector, will be more efficient. There may be a need for public regulation of emissions, but the generation methods should be left to industry. I do not believe the government is best at developing the means of energy generation, whether by windmills or solar energy. Let the government set goals and limits on air quality, but leave it to industry to devise the means to achieve the goals.

I consider myself a conservative on economic and business matters. As a rough rule, I believe the government that governs least governs best. On the other end of the spectrum are those considered liberals or progressives. They tend to favor a more activist public sector in matters of the economy and business. They often favor more prescriptive approaches to interacting with business. So, for example, liberals are more likely to embrace a climate change perspective and government policies mandating green solutions like solar and wind power for local electricity generation. Liberals promote a view of industry that says that profits incentivize greed and societally harmful practices.

I think liberals favor the Europeanizing of America. That's what I think my parents wanted to escape. I see Europe as gradually drifting toward an egalitarian form of society with an interventionist government directing the course. The government there has become increasingly activist in all matters of health care, the environment, regulation of business, and life, generally. I prefer a much less activist government, and I believe that stimulates competitive creativity that incentivizes economic growth.

On social matters, I don't see America as a racist or sexist society. It seems that folks of various races, sexes, and religions get along well. There are exceptions, I'm sure. Some white folks may not like Black folks, but then there are likely some Blacks who don't like whites. I do think the government has a role in ensuring that discrimination against any group in matters like education, employment, and housing is unlawful. But I don't think there should be any presumption that, as a general rule, discrimination other than on the basis of merit exists in our society. People, mostly in business, act out of self-interest. If someone is best qualified for a job, I think that person will get the job. Our country will be best served if we all embrace that old saying that the historically Black colleges used to use: "A mind is a terrible thing to waste." Seems like I haven't heard that expression in a long time.

13

MAYBE RETHINK REAL ESTATE INVESTING

I DID A LOT OF REAL ESTATE INVESTING OVER the years, and I see many younger folks getting into the business. In many cases, they're attracted to real estate because that investment allows them to control large amounts of capital using relatively safe leverage. But leverage could be a special problem in a hot market like in recent years. Remember that business cycle chart in Chapter 4, "Invest Only in Dividend Champions"? Markets will go down again, and real estate is not as liquid as securitized assets, which poses a special set of problems in a downdraft. I enjoyed real estate investing, and I was pretty good at it. But times changed, and there are much better options today.

Upon graduation from college, I moved to Washington, DC, to take a job with the government, and I attended Georgetown University Law School in the evenings. Tuition was still relatively low by today's standards, and my salary was a whole lot more than I'd made before, so I paid my tuition as I went along. After living expenses and tuition, I had very little capital. That's when I got bit by the real estate bug.

Growing up, my parents were apartment building superintendents in the Bronx. They did everything from renting the units to collecting the trash and mopping the halls. Each month, Mr. Loeb, the landlord, came to visit, and my mother met with him in the kitchen over tea and cookies, where they reviewed the rent rolls. My mom also showed Mr. Loeb her children's report cards. Sometimes I'd sit through the meeting, particularly if I had a good report card. And remember, that's where the cookies were. So, I had some familiarity with residential renting, and I got to understand Mr. Loeb's job as the owner.

My favorite board game as a child was Monopoly. I played it a lot. My pattern of play was always the same. Buy almost everything I landed on, and once I controlled a block of units, I'd start building houses, and eventually, hotels as soon as I could. My goal was to monopolize as much property as I could and start those rents flowing—not that different than in my adult life. Monopoly is a great board game to start the young entrepreneur out on.

Sometime after moving to DC, I got married, and we bought a two-unit townhouse in the far eastern region of Capitol Hill. It was a rough area, but the price was right. More importantly, the financing required no cash. There was an assumable first mortgage, and the seller took back a second mortgage for the balance. No cash down. The property needed renovation, and we moved into one of the units while doing the work. We took a personal loan from the credit union to finance the renovation, so we technically had three loans on the property.

We eventually renovated that building, moved to the suburbs, and continued to invest in residential real estate. We bought that early property for $18,000 and sold it a few years later for $36,000. A couple of years ago and about fifty years after our sale, it sold for $1.3 million. Some years later, when I considered how much time I put into the renovation, I realized I'd made very little per hour for my labor.

For many years after that first purchase and sale—and until the last ten years or so—I continued to buy, renovate, and develop rental property, both residential and commercial. I did that mostly out of habit; it's what I knew. I developed skills and relationships in that area and kept dealing in individual real estate investments. It helped that I always had ready access to relatively low-cost financing and was comfortable with significant leverage. In time and with the evolution of markets, I came to see things differently.

Personal Real Estate Investing Is Actually Running a Business

I did relatively well in my real estate ventures. I call those deals *personal real estate investing*. But over time, I started to see a sharp difference between running a business and investing. Many of my asset classes during my investing life have been securitized. That's particularly true with real estate and the advent of real estate investment trusts or REITs. I now view the securitized version of assets represented in the form of *stock* as the purer form of investing.

Today, you can own almost any form of real estate asset or real estate business in the form of a security. Owning assets in their raw, un-securitized state, whether it's a restaurant or real estate, is like running a business. Just as in owning a business, the effort and time required can be all consuming. It was for me. I did well in real estate largely because I worked so hard and long at it.

I often wonder how well I really did when you consider the capital I invested. But, perhaps more importantly, what was my real return when I consider all the time I spent acquiring, assembling, financing, and managing all those properties? What kind of return on investment did I actually achieve if I allotted myself only a minimum wage for all the time spent working? Then there was the wide range of skills I needed to acquire and maintain to run that business. Operating your own real estate investment business requires legal, financial, regulatory, construction, maintenance, repair, contractual, and other skills.

As I manage the succession process in our family—which is about my adult children and grandchildren succeeding me in managing the family asset management business—one thing is clear. My children are only too happy to take over the management of our securitized assets, but they have zero interest in managing personal real estate. None! No matter how I try to transfer my enthusiasm and skills to the next generation, there are no takers. I suspect they spent too much time watching Dad responding to fires and running hither and yon looking at deals, managing property, and dealing with banks, tenants, and partners. Child abuse!

But maybe the children's reaction to investing is rational. Being younger, they see more clearly the bifurcation between investment and business operations. Maybe they want to focus on investing and not be distracted by the time, energy, and capital required to run a business. The conversations go something like this: "Dad, so you like real estate? Let's look at the Dividend Champion REITs. On Justin's list this month, there are six Dividend Champion REITs. We're already considering them. If you need more, there are no fewer than forty-seven on Justin's most recent list of Challengers and Contenders that are making their way to Dividend Champion status." Sometimes I think I may have created a succession monster. No toilets, tenants, or trash—just investing.

From Real Estate Business to Investing

Over the last couple of years, we've sold a lot of our remaining real estate. I would like to say we timed it just right. The timing was part of it, but there were other reasons to sell, including all the work involved and no successors to handle that business. Virtually all the proceeds from recent real estate sales have gone into two things: paying taxes and purchasing Dividend Champions. Our family asset management business is increasingly about accumulating and managing highly liquid, securitized, dividend-growth businesses.

Hey, I still look at the occasional real estate deal. Guys call about deals, and what can I say, "My children don't want me to do this anymore"? Besides, old habits are tough to break. I call on ads, go to meetups, read market analyses, and talk to the guys I've dealt with for years. I still have the odd property and occasionally deal with managers, bankers, and tenants. I'm meeting a contractor this Monday to start reroofing a commercial building we still own. Next, we'll need to resurface the parking lot. This weekend, I'll buy the lady who purchased one of our last rental homes a new grapefruit tree. We took back a mortgage, and the tree we planted years ago recently died. Even after the sale, we shared the fruit. What am I supposed to do, not keep up my end? You get the picture. Personal real estate investing is high touch, and I like parts of that. But my overriding objective is to make my family rich, and there's only so much time and energy available. So, I may keep a hand in personal real estate, but it's becoming a hobby—maybe a profitable hobby, but a hobby. Look, some guys play golf. I suspect that takes more time than my dabbling in real estate.

Personal Real Estate vs. Dividend Champion REITs

With the advent of REITs and the significant expansion of REITs into a wide variety of real estate types, I think most investors are better off choosing REITs over personal real estate. There are exceptions, but the reasons for choosing REITs are many:

1. **Benefits of leverage without personal liability.** As in my early example of real estate investing, inexpensive financing tends to be readily available. For all practical purposes, the government effectively encourages real estate investing by providing not only support to residential mortgage markets but also significant tax advantages. That's what FNMA, GNMA, VA, and FHA are all about. But in many cases, if you borrow for investment purposes, you may have to pro-

vide a personal guarantee for the borrowing, thereby putting your entire net worth at risk. In fact, you may have liability for various personal injuries sustained at your property. Investing in real estate through a REIT involves no personal liability.

2. **REITs are completely passive.** There are no late-night calls and no management responsibilities. In my day, it seemed like there were never-ending calls from tenants, insurers, neighbors, agents, and bankers. There are no expenses to pay, detailed records to maintain, or special tax forms to prepare and file. By contrast, personal real estate is about as active as you can get, and the bookkeeping is extensive.

3. **REITs are liquid.** For the last couple of years, residential and some forms of commercial real estate have been hot. Homes have particularly been appreciating, and in many areas, multiple offers and bidding wars are common. As of this writing, a recession is looming, and mortgage rates are climbing. The stock market may be vulnerable and a downdraft will reduce the wealth effect that has fueled many of real estate's cash buyers. I expect real estate values to stabilize and decline. Personal real estate is not liquid. No matter how hot the market, real estate transactions are a cumbersome, time-consuming, and expensive process. REITs are like any other stock transaction: easy in and easy out.

4. **REIT investors pay no transaction costs.** REITs are like other stocks. There are either zero or minimal transaction fees. Starting with the usual 6% broker's fee and adding all the government transfer fees and title searches, the transaction costs for a personal real estate deal can run up to 10%. Less cost to buy, but still often 2% to 3% to include recording, mortgage origination, and title insurance.

5. **REITs are tax efficient.** You pay an income tax on your earnings and a capital gain when you sell with a profit—

just like owning other securitized investments. That's unlike personal real estate, where your property is periodically re-assessed by the local taxing authority. You also must maintain detailed records of expenses and depreciation on the improvements. Of course, you and your accounts will be subject to periodic audits by federal and state taxing authorities. The tax advantages of personal real estate can be a dangerous trap. That is largely because you can annually deduct depreciation from your income. Real estate depreciation is supposedly the annual amount you lose in value due to the aging of the improvements. Depreciation is not an actual cash cost, so it reduces the income you otherwise earn from your employment and investments. You will like that depreciation deduction when it comes time to prepare your taxes, but depreciation is dangerous. It accumulates year after year, and when you sell, it adds to the gain you must report. That is, it's a gain for which you do not receive any money but must pay capital gains as though you did receive the money.

There are several ways to reduce the tax effects of recovering depreciation and reducing your capital gains, but they are complex and costly. For example, you can structure your sale to exchange into a like-kind property. This so-called 1031 exchange shifts your taxable basis from the old property to the new property. Most recently, the government has allowed so-called Delaware Statutory Trusts or DSTs, where the seller can transfer his basis in the old property to participate in the ownership of multiple real estate properties. On a recent deal, an experienced broker who structured a number of 1031 and DST deals for clients estimated that the seller typically lost about 15% of the value he derived by requiring that he organize the sale as a tax-deferred exchange. You lose a lot of leverage and flexibility in the negotiating process when your objective is to minimize tax costs rather than maximize your gain. I've done 1031s in the past but will not in the future. I would rather pay Uncle Sam than take the reduction in return and prolong the pain. Generally, when I think it's time to move out of real estate, I don't want to exchange into other real estate.

6. **REITs allow wide diversification.** There are all kinds of REITs in terms of the kinds of property they accumulate. You can own REITs that specialize in everything from office buildings to quick-serve restaurants, government-leased buildings, data centers, and even billboards and farmland. Instead of concentrating your capital on a single or limited number of properties, you can diversify by type of property and location.

7. **REITs require a whole lot less time and effort.** To me, this is the single most important factor in my preference for REITs over owning individual property. I've spent enormous amounts of time acquiring, managing, refinancing, and selling my properties. If you want to focus on efficient investing and pursue the MYFR system, then invest in Dividend Champions, which can include some Dividend Champion REITs.

Some More Real Estate Stories

In my earlier book, *Make Your Family Rich: Why to Replace Retirement Planning with Succession Planning,* I included a chapter about real estate and related several anecdotes. Many readers, particularly those with personal real estate investing experience, found the stories humorous. Believe me; they were a whole lot funnier in the recounting than the living. Most of the stories depicted not only the range of skills required to successfully invest in personal real estate but also the vast amount of time required. Let me add to my repertoire of real estate stories by telling my recent experience with Frank Breen. By the way, that's a pseudonym to protect the innocent.

I own several apartments in the Washington, DC, area. Frank's firm had him on assignment there for a year or so, and he rented a unit from me in suburban Arlington County, Virginia. The property was managed for me by a very competent and efficient realtor; let's call her Kim. Frank's lease required that the property be professionally cleaned at the end of his lease. Frank apparently hired a cleaning service and then moved back to Missouri before inspecting the work. Kim arranged for the unit to be released, but when she showed up to review the apartment before the new tenant was to move in, the place was very dirty. Kim took lots of pictures. With the new tenant moving in the next day, Kim had to arrange a cleaning on very short notice at a cost of $425, which included cleaning carpets. The new tenant moved in without further incident, and Kim refunded Frank's security deposit less the $425.

That's when the fun began. In addition to posting very negative comments on Yelp and several similar platforms, Frank promptly filed a complaint against Kim with the state board of realtors. Then he filed a legal action in the local county court. After some legal wrangling and about $5,000 in legal fees for Kim's real estate firm, the judge advised Frank to file a suit against me as the owner. Frank represented himself in all these filings, including the suit against me. I'd been living in Texas but had moved back to Florida by the time Frank filed suit in Virginia. Frank supposedly gave notice of the suit at my former Texas address and proceeded with the suit in Arlington. Because I never received notice, I didn't appear for the trial in Virginia, and the court entered a default judgment against me for the $425 plus costs, which brought the total to about $800.

Frank then brought the Arlington judgment to my local Florida court, where I responded that I hadn't received notice, so the default judgment should not be executed. The Florida court agreed, and the case was set for trial, which, because of the pandemic, was held on Zoom. Frank, by this time, was a jailhouse lawyer and filed a long list of depositions and pleadings to which I had to respond. The trial day came, and Kim was ready to testify remotely. The judge did a professional job with Frank, who accused everyone of lying and accused Kim of being on the take from the cleaning service she arranged. Fortunately, the judge ruled in my favor. Months later, I received yet another demand from a collection agency for payment under the Arlington default judgment. This guy never quits.

Now you say, "Pat, you're nuts for spending this kind of time and money on a $425 claim." But where do you stop? When your manager has spent $5,000 to protect their liability and good name, do I throw in the towel and offer to pay the $800? Would Frank settle for the $800?

Then there was a local nonprofit. A couple of local guys and I did a renovate-to-suit for the organization. The deal was inked just before the pandemic hit. The transaction was a lease with a purchase option. The lease involved a base rent plus a supplemental rent to recover our cost for the renovation. The deal was agreed to the month before the pandemic struck, and the renovation costs went up by 60% once the virus took hold. Lumber costs alone increased by 150% during the pandemic. The lease provided that the construction cost risk was to be borne by the nonprofit tenant. When the property was completed, the tenant moved in and started paying the rent. By that time, the market had bounced back, and by my estimate, the tenant had a good lease and purchase deal, even with the increased renovation cost.

The nonprofit agency hired a new director who hired a local attorney on a pro bono basis to look into the deal. That's right; they were not paying the guy. He promptly advised them to stop paying rent. In fact, they paid the rent to their free attorney. We were forced to engage an attorney that was not free to bring an action for payment against this nonprofit. When they refused to pay, and as mortgage payments and other expenses came due, we filed for eviction. In Florida, mediation is required, and that usually involves hiring a retired judge or lawyer as a mediator.

We were effectively being blackmailed by the tenant occupying our building, refusing to pay rent and not incurring any legal expenses while our attorney fees and operating expenses mounted. Oh, but their free attorney did offer to send us a picture of the rent check. Nice guy. By the way, the owner-landlords, including me, had made zero dollars on the overage costs. It was to have been a simple pass-through to the tenant.

In the mediation, to stem the continuing legal costs, we agreed to absorb a significant portion of the overage. After lots of work, time, and cost, the shakedown was complete, and the tenant started paying the reduced rent. Then they promptly gave notice of their intent to exercise the purchase option. We, the owners, incurred legal costs and absorbed a portion of the overage. Our experience with this nonprofit illustrates the ways the legal system can be manipulated to disadvantage the owners and landlords of personal investment real estate.

You're vulnerable to these kinds of problems and inefficiencies when investing in personal real estate. Sure, you can make money and do well, but it's a lot of time and work. I believe you are better off in the securities markets buying great American Dividend Champion businesses. So, if you want some real estate coverage, it's there within the ranks of the Dividend Champions.

Proponents of personal real estate will argue that there are several advantages to individual ownership. For example, they'll say that you can leverage personal real estate. REITs leverage too. Advocates will also argue that personal real estate has the advantage of the depreciation deduction from taxable income. REITs have that opportunity, too, internal to the REIT. Then there's the opportunity to withdraw tax-free dollars from refinancing your property. REITs do that, too, again interior to the REIT. All the advantages of personal real estate are also advantages to REITs, but you do not have to do the work, develop the expertise, spend the time, or sustain all the personal risks.

If you get a chance, pick up a copy of *Make Your Family Rich: Why to Replace Retirement Planning With Succession Planning.* You'll get a kick out of the stories, and they may be enough to persuade you to skip personal real estate investing and move directly into the MYFR system of securities investing.

14

RETIREMENT? FERGEDABOUDIT!

K EEP AN OPEN MIND ABOUT THIS CHAPTER. Yes, I'm going to condemn the whole idea of convention- al retirement. It's just a scam perpetrated by a bunch of socialists to put a spin on their numbers. Think about it. The Great Depression was raging, and nothing was working to reverse the un- employment rolls. So, FDR invented retirement. Those older guys were no longer unemployed; they were now retired. Then he had to invent Social Security to fund all those old unemployed, sorry, retired guys. Then along came World War II, and that finally ended the Depression. It was Tojo and Hitler who finally ended the De- pression. Anyway, that's my story, and I'm sticking to it.

The FINER Life

To me, it makes no sense to retire. This book should prove to you that it will make no sense to you either. But if you have your heart set on all that fishing, golf, traveling, and time with the family schtick, no problem. You'll get that done in an infinitely better and more satisfying way. Just stick with me and keep an open mind because we're going to refute all that conventional retirement thinking. That thinking, by the way, is not only wrong, but it's also not good for your health, longevity, or your family's well-being.

That's right. This chapter is going to introduce you to living the FINER life. We've all heard about the FIRE acronym—Financial Independence Retire Early. Lots of financial advisers push that as an objective for their clients. Those financial advisor guys are all the same with their catchy phrases and acronyms. How about the guy who says the worst thing that can happen in your retirement is to run out of money? Is he nuts? Look, I'm a spouse, a brother, a parent, and a grandparent. I'm also an American and a Republican. Do you want something worse than running out of money? How about a terminally sick child or grandchild or a close friend or relative who's disabled with some form of addiction, and you don't have the financial wherewithal to help? How about another pandemic but one that's started in an American lab? Even worse is the Democrats capturing the presidency, both Houses of Congress, and gaining a majority in the Supreme Court. Don't get me started. Running out of money in retirement? That guy, Ken Fisher, has not been exposed to the Financial Independence Never Ever Retire (FINER) life.

Let's start with Warren Buffett. As of this writing, the guy is ninety-two, and someone just paid $19 million to have lunch with him. That didn't even include his partner, Charlie Munger. Ready for this? Charlie is ninety-nine. Those two guys are still working to build their business, which is mostly their interest in Berkshire Hathaway, a conglomerate of great American businesses. Few talk about Buffett's or Munger's retirement plans. In fact, it might be hard to find an investor in Berkshire who wants them to retire. Mostly all the age-related conversations about Warren and Charlie pertains to who will succeed them.

That's the way you want it to be with your asset management business. You keep working at it, but your successors get increasingly proficient, ready to step into your shoes when you are gone. You stay active, and the next generation gets trained to seamlessly step into leadership when the time comes. Retirement? Don't be silly. You just keep doing what you've always done, maybe spending a bit less time at it if that's what you want. However it works for you, it's your job to train, nurture, and incentivize your successors, just like Warren and Charlie. That's the FINER life: Financial Independence Never Ever Retire.

Our FINER Life

Let's talk about the succession plan for my family. For several years, Matt and Erin have been exposed to the logic, structure, and operations of the Make Your Family Rich system. In speaking to other folks about the system, I frequently hear, "But my children aren't interested in investments." Well, no kidding. I hear it all the time. Do you think a twelve-year-old thinks reading the *Wall Street Journal* or tuning in to CNBC is their idea of a good time?

Having tutored my children and grands throughout their education, I've created Pat's First Rule of Mathematics and Economics. I just call it *Pat's First Rule*. That is, let's say a child's effort to learn math is "x." That's the measure of the time, energy, and interest a youngster wants to spend learning math and economics. Pat's First Rule says, "A youngster's effort is reduced to x/2 if all the numbers used to instruct the child have dollar signs in front of them." Don't labor over it too much; it's just the way it is. But here's the real power of Pat's First Rule. If the child believes it's their money, then the effort and time expended in learning become x/4. You got it. Those little devils learn four times faster and better if it's not only about money but *their* money. Don't fight Pat's First Rule. Just accept it and apply it to your training and succession on the path to make your family rich and your FINER life. It takes a while for Pat's First Rule to take hold. But if you stick with it, you'll see the lights turn on, and that can be very satisfying. So, forget the "my children are not interested in investments" nonsense.

Here's how I transferred my knowledge. My first book was really the training manual for Matt and Erin. Therein, I detailed the origins, logic, and approach to the MYFR system. Then I started

paying them a monthly fee. If they were going to spend time training and discussing the system, then it would be appropriate to compensate them. They both have jobs and were paid for their time
and effort there, so they should be paid for their time and effort
in becoming proficient in the MYFR system. See those dollar signs
working their way in? Furthermore, once they were on the payroll,
they were anxious to earn the money. Don't fight that. Just accept it
for now.

Our Prior Financial Relationship

A good amount of our family capital was managed by David Love
at Davenport Securities in Virginia. I initially started working
with David years ago because he had great access to thinly traded bonds when rates were higher. For example, David could access
$20K worth of mortgage-backed Jewish nursing home bonds in the
Maryland suburbs of Washington, DC. Who does that? Well, David did. How about Lutheran retirement home bonds in McLean,
VA? Then there were Yankee Stadium bonds. David and his firm
always seemed to have access to smaller lots of fixed income and
often tax-free securities on well-secured but not-real-liquid bonds.
For the most part, I think the securities came out of the estates of old
Virginia families. David and Davenport had a great niche; plus, he
and his assistant, Christy Rose, were a delight to deal with.

Over the years, as rates came down, I migrated the David account to the MYFR system. But I told David that I planned to move
the account to Erin and or Matt if they ever developed proficiency
in the MYFR system. Look, if you come to like the MYFR system
but don't want to do it yourself, David and Christy are great. If they
apply the MYFR system on your behalf, I believe their standard
financial advisory fees will be more than covered by the options premiums they generate for you. I once asked David why he wasn't routinely buying stock for his other clients by selling out-of-the-money
cash-backed puts. In response, David said he simply could not get

most clients informed and comfortable with the system. That represents my own observations of even long-term investors. They have a negative, stereotypical reaction to options. But if this book gets you sold on the MYFR system and put option sales, the team of David and Christy can certainly implement the system for you.

Matt and Erin Start to Take Over

Let's get back to Matt and Erin. Both were good students with solid math skills. Matt's math was somewhat intuitive; Erin's was more learned and disciplined. They got to the same place but by different routes. The only reason I mention that is that no two people are the same. You should fight the temptation to prefer dealing with an individual because I think that with time, you'll find that the skills are complementary, and your application of the MYFR system will be stronger and more valuable the more freedom you afford your successors.

Matt, like several people I've met along the way, had a negative opinion of options. He associated trading options with risk and debt—neither one of which he had an appetite for. I find this attitude somewhat common, and I think it has to do with more exotic forms of options than we use. I think it also has to do with buying options, which we never do. We never lose money selling options because the option either expires as worthless and we keep the premium, or we buy the stock at a reduced price. That's the win-win deal we like.

As discussed in Chapter 5, "Sell the Dips; Out-of-the-Money *Put Options*, That Is," options come with their own language that can be difficult to grasp. In some ways, it's even more difficult for the individual who has experience investing in stocks. That's because the options vocabulary has different meanings for the same words, as in stock trading. Take, for example, the way we typically buy an interest in a business. We don't buy a stock when it dips; we sell a put option when a Dividend Champion dips in the hope of eventually buying the stock should the option expire below the strike price. It's frequently the case in training an individual on the MYFR system that even after some experience, the prospective investor will continue to refer to "buying a put" when they mean "selling a put." It's just hard to change habits. Folks have been steeped in the advantages of buying dips, and that has formed the language they use, and now they must learn how to use the same words differently. It can be a struggle.

I trained both Matt and Erin for several months before setting them off on their own to manage the account. When I did that, I closed the account with Davenport and merged that with my long-standing TD Ameritrade account. I set some limits on the extent of options selling, and with that, Matt and Erin started to manage the family business. At about that time, I concentrated on marketing our real estate assets to generate more capital for the asset management business now operated by Matt and Erin. Most of our property was either in the Washington, DC, area or in Florida, where we live. As property sales settled, the money was transferred to the account managed by Matt and Erin. They continued to sell puts and generated a nice cash flow, resulting in some Dividend Champion purchases. Matt and Erin were being paid at the same 1% annual rate I'd been paying David Love's firm. They were paid quarterly, and the monthly stipend already being paid to them became part of their overall management fees. Are you starting to see the effort and time required to get over the "my children aren't interested" thing?

For a considerable period, the management fees didn't cost the business or me anything. That's because the options premiums Matt and Erin were generating more than covered their management expense. Each day Matt and Erin checked the Dividends Champion list on Yahoo Finance and sold puts on the businesses that had dipped the most. There were some exceptions. For example, because we own so many community banks in the Washington, DC, area, they didn't sell options on Dividend Champion banks. Community banks on the Dividend Champion list tend to be relatively thinly traded and either don't offer options or have very wide bid and ask prices, which make it difficult to trade efficiently. So, excluding community banks made sense for us.

The Evolution of the Multigenerational Management

I've never been confident in the Biden Administration. I didn't like his early energy restrictions, and I certainly didn't like the nature of his appointments. In the appointments, I saw an anti-business bias that was significantly different from the prior administration. With the disastrous withdrawal from Afghanistan in the late summer of 2021, I lost even more confidence in the Biden Administration's ability to provide leadership.

Years ago, it was common for financial analysts to discuss and factor political risk into their international investment recommendations. In recent years, the moves to promote global investing tended to ignore any consideration of political risk. But I was beginning to see significant political risk in our country. This is particularly important to our MYFR system because we almost exclusively invest in those long-term dividend-increasing great American companies that are Dividend Champions.

I don't like the whole idea of market timing. Markets go through expansions and recessionary retractions, and that's just the way our economy works. But, in my view, the Biden Administration was seriously mishandling the national economy and our position in the world. This was at a time when the national debt was more than $30 trillion, making our currency and economy particularly vulnerable, in my opinion. With energy prices also increasing and affecting the price of virtually everything, I started to become especially concerned about inflation. Initially, I had no idea how the Federal Reserve Bank would handle a steep increase in inflation when, historically, the Fed's practice and statutory mandate had been to raise rates to quell growth, thereby supposedly helping to extinguish inflationary fires. But raising rates with such a huge debt created enormous uncertainty in my mind. Currently, the war in Ukraine continues with no certainty as to its end, injecting yet another uncertainty and destabilizing factor into the world's markets.

With all this uncertainty as a backdrop, we sold much of our real estate and closed in late 2021 and early 2022. Until the first of 2022, we'd been trading mostly as usual, with Matt and Erin selling puts on dips and occasionally buying more stock in the Dividend Champions. Their guidelines, until that time, limited them to options sales up to a maximum potential debt or margin of 20%. That is, if every put is executed on expiration, then the total margin incurred could not exceed 20% of the equity of our business.

Early in 2022, with the additional risk of an expanding European war looming, we started meeting together to discuss the risk environment and the condition of our business, including the availability of cash reserves. Those cash reserves were mostly the proceeds from the recent real estate sales. By the way, having sold so much real estate, we were facing a significant tax bill, so we had to hold back funds to pay our taxes. With all of that on the agenda, we agreed to back down to 10% on the amount of potential margin we could incur.

A month or so later, with the Ukrainian war ongoing and inflation and interest rates increasing, we changed guidelines again. We kept with the 10% limit but further restricted put selling to days when the Dow was down at least 800 points on no more than two consecutive days. We further restricted trading to a limit of one contract on each business for any Dividend Champion declining at least 3% and with strike prices at least 15% below the market price at the time the put was sold. Finally, options were not to be sold with expirations more than ninety days into the future.

By late spring 2022, inflation was increasing, and interest rates continued to rise. The Biden Administration still refused to increase domestic energy exploration and production, and the Ukrainian war continued. Things still did not look good, and the political wrangling continued to intensify with the House of Representatives Democrat-run January sixth proceedings that further fueled conflict and national division. The employment market kept strong into the summer of 2022, but with the stock market down and interest rates up significantly, the real estate market was starting to show signs of stress. Unemployment was still low, but where else was there good news to fuel a resurgent market?

All of this is meant to show how managing our family asset management business continues to evolve on a multigenerational basis. Our tools are relatively fixed, but how and when we deploy them can be changed. Matt, Erin, and I act somewhat like a board of directors that discusses and collectively decides on changes to our implementation. We have what seems like a productive division of labor. We never discussed that in detail, but it has evolved.

Matt and Erin do the trading within board guidelines. Matt seems to take primary responsibility for the spreadsheet design, and he and Erin trade off periodically in the actual management of the spreadsheet. Erin has set up and manages the www.makeyourfamilyrich.com website, and I lead the board's deliberations and try to stay informed on market events. I also prepare most of the written material posted on the website. It seems like a positive working relationship that provides quality multigenerational leadership for our family asset management business.

Matt and Erin recently received a 10% raise to 1.10% annually of the average value of the business paid quarterly. The raise made sense, given their expanding role and skills. With their design of risk management spreadsheets and website management, they provided more service than the standard financial advisor.

Enter Another Generation

Then there are the grandchildren. Years ago, I set up separate funds for them, and I made contributions on their birthdays and Christmas. Initially, the intended purpose was to fund their advanced education. I continue to personally manage the grandchildren's accounts, and I also manage my personal IRA. In time, I expect to transfer the management of those accounts to Matt and Erin or to the grandchildren themselves. I discuss the accounts as the grandchildren's businesses, much like our family business. Their business is to own a variety of Dividend Champions, and the only time businesses should be sold is if they lose their Dividend Champion status by failing to increase dividends or if money is needed to fund that other great investment—their higher education.

I now report to the grandchildren every month on the status of their businesses and how I've been managing things. I'm introducing them to the math of options selling and DRIPping. Appendix C shows a couple of those monthly letters. It's like everything else when dealing with youngsters. You pass through the early eye-rolling phase into the uh-huh kind of "that's what Pop does" phase and eventually into the asking questions phase when Pat's First Rule takes hold. As they come to think of it as *their* business and *their* money, the learning and interest accelerate. It's my hope that one day, they'll take over their own businesses and eventually evolve into participating with their parents in the overall family asset management business.

I've also opened the prospect with Matt and Erin that the grandchildren might eventually want to merge their businesses into the larger family asset management business. That could be easy enough to figure out. Simply take the value of the various accounts or businesses on the given merger day, and the merged account value buys a proportionate share of the larger family asset management business.

I still own the grands' accounts and reserve the right to manage them as I think serves the best interest of the young people. It's still my money. My priority will be the education and well-being of the young people.

My second book, *Hey Kid! Wanna Own Great American Businesses?* was targeted at educating the young investor and introducing him or her to the MYFR system. I thought of it as the training manual for my teen grandchildren, somewhat like *Make Your Family Rich: Why to Replace Retirement Planning with Succession Planning* was the training manual for my adult children. *Hey Kid!* has much of the substance of the earlier book but none of the options discussions. Instead, I discuss the magic of buying slices of individual Dividend Champions. Can you imagine Mrs. Market making things any easier for youngsters to get started early in owning businesses than offering slices of businesses with no trading commissions?

My FINER Life Today

I don't have a regular paying job, and I can work as little or as much as I want. But I want to work a lot doing the stuff I've always done— at least as a part-time gig. Now it's mostly full-time or as full-time as I want it to be. Plus, I'm dealing with the people I care about the most, helping provide them with security and well-being. That's what parents are supposed to do, and in their own way, that's what my parents did for their family. I could have developed a great big Italian restaurant and progressed the children through the ranks of polishing silverware, prepping in the kitchen, bussing tables, waiting on customers, and managing the front or back of the house to eventual ownership. But the world changed during my lifetime. Pretty much everything got securitized, and the role of investor became more clearly bifurcated from business owner and manager.

If your objective is to create wealth and make your family rich, then the best approach is to focus on the role of investor and train your family in how to manage that investment business. In a way, the progress through our family asset management business is not that different than progressing through that imaginary big Italian restaurant. But I'm of Irish descent, and we don't do Italian or any other restaurants—and my father always advised us to stay away from any business that focused on booze. You know, bars and liquor stores. Recently, I was offered the opportunity to rent a building we own to a retail marijuana or cannabis chain. Great location and a neat building that I developed a couple of years back. The old man never said anything about not being involved in marijuana, but my suspicion is that since he felt so strongly about not being in the booze business, he wouldn't want his family renting to a marijuana retailer. I turned the deal down even when the fellow continued to up his offered rent.

You get the picture. Why would I ever consider retiring? I'm the Warren Buffett of our family asset management business. I'm providing for my succession, but in the meantime, I'm chairman of the family business. Retirement? Fergedaboudit! I chose the FINER life, and I think you would like it, too.

APPENDIX A:
YAHOO FINANCE SAMPLE

Search for news, symbols or companies

My Watchlist DCs

Symbol	Last Price	Change	Chg %	Currency	Market Time	Volume	Shares	Avg Vol (3m)	Day Range		52-Wk Range		Day Chart	Market Cap
FELE	96.75	+6.22	+6.87%	USD	4:00PM EDT	373,460	-	177,506	89.60	97.81	68.38	100.00		4.472B
ECL	174.28	+5.50	+3.26%	USD	4:03PM EDT	1.793M	-	1.161M	167.66	174.52	131.04	178.06		49.612B
LEG	32.32	+0.95	+3.03%	USD	4:00PM EDT	1.317M	-	892,490	31.70	33.50	30.05	41.94		4.301B
EFSI	32.50	+0.50	+1.56%	USD	9:58AM EDT	300	-	776	32.00	32.50	28.00	38.40		114.493M
MSA	132.43	+2.01	+1.54%	USD	4:00PM EDT	285,348	-	103,148	122.57	133.03	108.75	146.33		5.193B
WST	369.62	+3.49	+0.95%	USD	4:03PM EDT	341,715	-	546,380	364.48	370.60	206.19	372.06		27.452B
JNJ	165.03	+1.43	+0.87%	USD	4:00PM EDT	7.497M	-	8.025M	163.56	165.46	150.11	183.35		514.867B
BMI	137.66	+1.11	+0.81%	USD	4:00PM EDT	144,338	-	144,203	135.33	138.66	73.20	139.33		4.035B
CWT	55.81	+0.35	+0.63%	USD	4:00PM EDT	266,549	-	230,146	54.62	56.08	48.46	66.12		3.125B
RPM	81.81	+0.46	+0.57%	USD	4:00PM EDT	663,801	-	635,810	79.98	81.87	74.56	106.50		10.546B
AWR	88.42	+0.41	+0.47%	USD	4:00PM EDT	117,160	-	159,346	86.80	88.73	71.22	100.51		3.269B
ROP	460.72	+2.09	+0.46%	USD	4:03PM EDT	656,952	-	569,243	456.60	463.70	356.22	466.26		49.083B
PNR	57.85	+0.24	+0.42%	USD	4:03PM EDT	1.253M	-	1.542M	56.36	57.91	38.55	60.85		9.542B
CLX	167.72	+0.60	+0.36%	USD	4:00PM EDT	1.632M	-	1.168M	166.13	168.17	120.50	168.72		20.718B
DCI	64.56	+0.23	+0.36%	USD	4:00PM EDT	480,150	-	440,815	63.39	64.62	46.00	66.98		7.83B
PEP	192.25	+0.57	+0.30%	USD	4:00PM EDT	3.536M	-	4.46M	189.77	192.50	164.56	192.50		264.861B
CL	80.85	+0.16	+0.20%	USD	4:00PM EDT	5.75M	-	4.49M	80.26	81.06	67.84	63.81		67.278B
NDSN	217.92	+0.39	+0.18%	USD	4:00PM EDT	226,007	-	232,766	215.05	218.25	194.89	251.26		12.478B

APPENDIX B: PERSONAL FINANCIAL STATEMENT (PFS)

John J. Smith
1074 Summit Avenue
Miami, Florida 68342
918.632.xxxx
johnjsmith12@internet.com

FINANCIAL STATEMENT
October 31, 2019

I. CASH	$135,000
II. STOCKS & BONDS	$5,098,853
III. REAL ESTATE	$1,535,000
IV. PARTNERSHIPS	$2,088,582
V. RETIREMENT	$891,000
VI. OTHER	$38,000
TOTAL ASSETS	$9,786,435
TOTAL LIABILITIES	$1,042,266
NET WORTH	$8,744,169

10.65%
%LIABILITIES/ASSETS

John J. Smith   3.31.19
JOHN J. SMITH   DATE

ASSETS

I. CASH			$135,000
A. PERSONAL	I-1	$95,000	
B. CERTIFICATES OF DEPOSIT	I-2	$40,000	

II. SECURITIES			$5,098,853
A. ABC BROKERAGE	II-1	$3,972,000	
B. DEF BROKERAGE	II-2	$1,126,853	

III. REAL ESTATE			$1,535,000
A. 106 OAK ST.	III-1	$385,000	
B. 1210 WALNUT ST.	III-2	$280,000	
C. 642 SYCAMORE AVE.	III-3	$495,000	
D. 342 8TH AVE	III-4	$375,000	

ASSETS

IV. PARTNERSHIPS					$2,088,582
	INTEREST	MKT VALUE	LOAN	NET	
A. DPM PARTNERS					
1. MORT NOTES IV A-1	50.00%	$320,000	$0	$160,000	
2. LAND IV A-2	50.00%	$150,000	$540,000	$75,000	
B. FAIRFAX PARTNERS IV B	40.00%	$1,700,000	$295,000	$464,000	
C. FAIRFAX PARTNERS 2 IV C	33.00%	$600,000	$550,000	$305,000	
D. MCLEAN OFFICE PARTNERS IV D	33.30%	$804,000	$1,130,000	$84,582	
E. DC WAREHOUSES IV E	40.00%	$2,300,000	$0	$468,000	
F. 3750 10TH ST NE IV G	50.00%	$750,000	$465,000	$375,000	
G. LOFTON CREEK PLAZA IV H	20.00%	$1,250,000		$157,000	
TOTALS		$7,874,000	$2,980,000	$2,088,582	

V. RETIREMENT			$891,000
A. STATE RETIREMENT SYSTEM	V-1	$250,000	
B. IRA	V-2	$641,000	

VI. OTHER			$38,000
A. CARS	VI-1	$33,000	
B. PERSONAL	VI-2	$5,000	

TOTAL ASSETS $9,786,435

LIABILITIES

A. MORTGAGES			$665,949
1. 106 OAK ST.	$109,990	A-1	
2. 1210 WALNUT ST	$109,990	A-2	
3. 642 SYCAMORE AVE.	$304,639	A-3	
4. 342 8TH AVE	$141,330	A-4	
TOTAL	**$665,949**		

B. MARGIN		$376,317
1. ABC BROKERAGE	$376,317	

TOTAL LIABILITIES $1,042,266

NET WORTH $8,744,169

APPENDIX C:
LETTERS TO MY GRANDSON

9.30.22

Hi Mike:

Back home in Florida. Great seeing you and your Mom, and thanks a lot for coming to visit us at the new place in Llano. That place is for all of us, so I hope you make use of it. Folks in Llano are very friendly, and I think more folks from Austin and other cities will make their way out there over time. The only problem is they close the library on Saturday. What's with that? But they left the Wi-Fi on for me so I could work in the parking lot. We'll get all that straightened out at the house soon and get you a bed, etc., too.

Just saw your month-end September statement. The good news is your estimated annual income went up from $4,083.38 at the end of August to $4,091.68 at the end of September. You have two companies out on options. You have a 10.21 call on T, and it probably will expire unexecuted, so you can sell another call. You also have a 10.21 put of MSFT that looks like you might buy at $240. That's a great company that has paid an increasing dividend for twenty years. That's longer than you have been around. The MSFT dividend has increased by 13% per year for the last ten years, compounding at 13%/year; imagine what it will be paying you when you are thirty-five!

The bad news is the value of your business over the month dropped from $134,372.31 to $117,438.37. It was a bad month for values, but we measure success mostly by income. That's because income is something we can control by sticking to Dividend Champions. The market goes up, and it comes down, and we can't control that. But over my lifetime, markets always come back. Sometimes it takes years, but it comes back, and you have lots of years to be patient.

The other good news is that markets have dropped a lot, so your dividend yields are up. That is, if the denominator (the price of the company) goes down and the numerator (dividend) stays the same or goes up, then your percent return increases. Capice? The other good news is with markets down, we can sell puts at lower prices, so if you buy the stock, your prices will be lower.

Remember, the options expiration for you is Oct 21 on both T and MSFT. Sure hope you get to buy MSFT and add it to the businesses you already own. Maybe you and your mom can check the account at the close on 10.21 and see if you bought MSFT and sold T. I love options expirations Fridays.

The elections are coming in November. As a rough rule, Republicans tend to believe and have confidence in markets. That is, left to their own devices, businesses will design the best tools. Democrats tend to think that government knows best and can better dictate how markets and people should behave. So, Republicans tend to be more business friendly and better for markets, in my opinion. By the way, it looks like most folks out in Llano are pretty conservative and Republican. See you soon in Llano.

Love, Pop

7.31.22

Hi Mike:

How about those parents? Fishing trips in Colorado and all these trips to San Antonio for baseball games. Wow!

You had a good month in Mike's business. Your business owns a bunch of great American businesses that pay a regular and increasing income to your business. That income is called dividends, and your dividends are constantly increasing. The only better investment than these great American businesses you own is your higher education. Got that? The best investment ever is your higher education. That's college and then graduate school, depending on what you plan to do.

We measure our success mostly by our income. That's the main way we keep score. This is not going to happen every month, but your income increased from an estimated annual amount of $3,796.65 at the end of June to $4,031.42 at the end of July. That's an increase of 6.18% for the month or 74.2% for the year. That is very rare. The value of your business went from $125,678.94 to $141,064.42 or increased by 12.2%. Remember, you don't control the value. The market goes up and down, and we can't do much about that. But we can control income by picking only businesses that increase your dividends. Those businesses are called Dividend Champions, and those are 143 businesses that have increased dividends for at least twenty-five years. Think about that. These businesses have been increasing their owners' income for almost twice as long as you have been alive! The folks that run these businesses are All Stars.

You had a lot of DRIPs during the month. That stands for Dividend Reinvestment Plan. That's where you get more stock instead of getting cash dividends. Later that means even more dividends because you own more of the business. You had DRIPs on ITW (Illinois Tool Works), CAH (Cardinal Health Care), BEN (Franklin

Fund), and LAND (Gladstone Land). LAND is the only one that's not a Dividend Champion. It owns a lot of farmlands around the country and pays a nice increasing dividend. It has not been around for twenty-five years yet. By the way, it's headquartered in McLean, where your Mom and Dad grew up. We call businesses like that STIs or Scratch the Itch businesses. They are not Dividend Champions yet, but we think they will be, given enough time. Kind of like being in the minor leagues batting 350. You know he's going to the bigs, but you just aren't sure exactly when.

You sold thirty-five shares of WBD, which you received in a spinoff from T. WBD does not pay any dividends. Hasta la vista, WBD. You had sold a call on your T, which is no longer a Dividend Champion, having reduced its dividend. The call expired in July, so you sold another call this month and received $42.54. Because T is no longer a Dividend Champion, we unDRIPped T, and you received the dividend in cash. Your mom understands all that, so she can explain better. You will understand it soon, too. You will be the only guy at your high school that digs this stuff. Maybe you could sell a couple of my teen books.

Love, Pop

12.31.22

Hi Mike:

On the road back to Free Florida. Got your month-end Dec 2022 data, so figured I'd use the time to write your month and year-end (2022) report. My new book (*Live the FINER Life, Financial Independence Never Ever Retire*) is with the editors, and a couple of your month-end letters are appendices to the book. Don't worry; I changed your name to Mike. The letters are there to illustrate the process needed to get future generations informed on how to run their businesses. Kind of like your mom and Uncle Matt do now, running the family business.

There was some good news in Nov. with the Republicans taking control of the House of Representatives. Maybe they can help control the Democrats' spending. The growing national debt is scary and a threat to the US economy and businesses. By the way, some of those are "Mike's businesses." Mike's businesses will do better in a healthy economy not threatened by huge government debt.

So much for my political propaganda. On to your details. At the end of 2022, Mike's Business had a market value of $133,792.88 and was earning you an estimated $2,620.45/year. The overall market during 2022 was down about 20% on the Standard and Poor's Index and about 10% on the DOW Industrial average. So, by the way most folks (not us) calculate things, that was a terrible year. One of the worst. We added $12,000 in capital to Mike's Business in 2022. If nothing had changed, your business would be worth $145,792.88 at year-end 2022. In fact, Mike's Business was worth $140,231.98. So, you were down 4.6%. Now make sure you are sitting down. Your estimated annual income at the end of Dec 2022 is $4,189.62. That's an increase of 59.9% from year-end 2021! That's a great year for Mike's Business. Imagine if that happened every year. Then remember all that income is being used to expand Mike's Business by DRIPping. Your mom understands everything about DRIPping. DRIPping is the next best thing to a grand slam in the bottom of the ninth when you are behind eight to five. So, you were buying more shares during a year when the prices of those shares were going down a lot. It's okay to take a short time out and sing a chorus from God Bless America.

On a monthly basis, your business value at the end of November 2022 was $148,539.92 earning $4,138.56. So, you were actually up for the year through November. But down a lot in value during December, but even then, you were way up on your income. Value? Fergedaboudit! You can't control what the market does, but you can and do control your income by making sure Mike's Business invests only in those great American businesses, Dividend Champions.

I will be adding your Christmas present once I get home. Next month, I'll fill you in on what we do with the new capital. You can go over the details of your transactions with your mom on your December statement.

One of these days, you will be running Mike's Business, and your Mom understands this stuff, including the trading of options to generate additional income and buy the great Dividend Champions.

Remember, one of the priorities for Mike's Business is to invest in the owner's (Mike's) higher education. That's your best investment. Part of that is to help Mike lead a life of freedom to make the choices best for you.

Great seeing you at the Llano house. The beds for your room are supposed to be delivered soon. Hope to see you soon again. Did you see the great cowboy clock your mom got me for Christmas? Love that clock. It's in my Llano office. Got a battery for it before I left, but I still have to hang it properly. Happy New Year!

Love,
Pop

2.28.23

Hi Mike:

Hope all is going well in school. Heard you made the baseball team. Congratulations!

Your business had a good January. Your estimated annual income increased from $4,189.62 at the end of December 2022 to $4,225.76 at the end of January 2023. That's an annualized rate of increase of 10.4%. Nice rate of increase. The market value of your business went from $140,231.96 to $154,287.39 for an increase of 10% for the month. But that was affected partially by the $5,000 Christmas present Fran and I added. But taking that out, you were still up 6.5%.

Remember, the MYFR system keeps score by income. Markets go up, and they go down, and you can't control that. But you can control your income by investing only in Dividend Champions. So long as your income is constantly increasing, your values will increase over time. Just trust me on that one. I've been doing this for a long time. Now you see why you want to be good at math. When you're investing and running an investment business like your mom, Uncle Matt, and I are—and you will be—it's all about math. So, make sure you stay sharp in math. It's something you will use pretty much every day in your life.

You had eleven DRIPs during the month. That means that in lieu of dividends, you received an increased interest in the businesses you own. Tell me how cool that is. Eleven! You also paid some margin interest. Not sure how you got a margin account, but it allows you to borrow to buy businesses. I don't like using margin and did not do it intentionally. As we sell puts, we can use the income to pay the margin off. Not a good idea for you to be borrowing, and it's more expensive today because rates have been going up, and margin accounts increase with market rates.

Remember, building your business is all about creating freedom and independence in your life and for your family and anyone who depends on you. It's not about buying stuff. How much stuff do you really need? It's all about getting the education you want and need and acquiring the wealth to let you lead the life you want to live.

You may want to look at your account statement with your mom to see how things have been going. Do check out those eleven DRIPs. You remember what **DRIP** stands for, right? Fortunately, you have your mom right there, and she digs all this stuff.

I just got back from Orlando. I was there for about four days, going to school about managing city pension fund investments. I'm on the city pension board for Gainesville, Florida, which is the home of the University of Florida. All the cops, firefighters, and other city employees have pension plans for when they get older, and five guys, including me, manage the investments that will pay those pensions. So, like you, we have a whole lot of great businesses (total value is now $700 million!) working to create wealth to pay all these people when they are old. Anyway, I love doing the work, but every so often, I have to go to school and take tests to show I still have my lights on. Back when I was your age and was always taking tests, I wasn't really keen on that. Now I really like the schools, the tests, and working for and with all those cops and firefighters. Maybe you can talk your mom into doing it in Texas. Or maybe one day you or your brother will be doing this work.

See you soon.

Love,

Pop

ABOUT THE AUTHOR

Patrick J. Keogh was once in charge of the family office that handles the assets of the Keogh family, but he has passed those responsibilities on to his children, Matt and Erin. The office holds securities of the kind recommended in this book. The office also manages a portfolio of real estate assets, but over time, they are migrating that real estate to Dividend Champions. He still does an occasional development deal. Old habits are tough to break.

Pat was born, raised, and educated in the Bronx. He started work at age fourteen, selling hot dogs and peanuts for Harry M. Stevens Inc. at Yankee Stadium and other area sports venues. His professional career was focused as a financial and real estate development executive with the US General Services Administration. He left government service in 1994 and went into private practice, specializing in public-private partnerships for development projects. Pat is a certified pension trustee and was chairman of the board of a Florida municipal pension plan. He is a graduate of Manhattan College in the Bronx and the Georgetown University Law Center night school in Washington, DC. Pat is a member of the Virginia Bar and the American Association of Individual Investors.

To contact the author, email pjakeogh@gmail.com.

For more information about the Make Your Family Rich system, visit www.makeyourfamilyrich.com, and look for Erin and Matt's Daily Diary.